All English Accents Matter

Orelus' valuable study draws on the scholarly work of sociocultural and postcolonial theorists, as well as testimonies collected from study participants, to explore accentism, the systemic form of discrimination against speakers whose accents deviate from a socially constructed norm.

Orelus examines the manner in which accents are acquired and the effects of such acquisition on the learning and educational experiences of linguistically and culturally diverse students. He goes on to demonstrate the ways in which, and the degree to which, factors such as race, class, and country of origin are connected with nonstandard accent-based discrimination. Finally, this book proposes alternative ways to challenge and counter the accentism that minority groups, including linguistically and culturally diverse groups, have faced in schools and in society at large.

It will be of interest to all of those concerned with linguistic/accent-based prejudice and the experience of those who face it.

Dr. Pierre Wilbert Orelus is an associate professor at Fairfield University and past Chair of the Educational Studies and Teacher Preparation Department, where he is the director of the Teaching and Foundation master's program. His research is intersectional, examining ways in which race, language, and class interweave to affect people's lives in general and student learning in particular, often in ways that go unnoticed. His most recent books include *Unschooling Racism* (2020) and *How It Feels to Be Black in the USA* (2022).

Routledge Studies in Sociolinguistics

Titles include:

The Sociolinguistics of Global Asias
Edited by Jerry Won Lee

Implicit and Explicit Language Attitudes
Mapping Linguistic Prejudice and Attitude Change in England
Robert M. McKenzie and Andrew McNeill

Negotiating Linguistic and Religious Diversity
A Tamil Hindu Temple in Australia
Nirukshi Perera

Social and Regional Variation in World Englishes
Local and Global Perspectives
Edited by Paula Rautionaho, Hanna Parviainen, Mark Kaunisto, and Arja Nurmi

Everyday Multilingualism
Linguistic Landscapes as Practice and Pedagogy
Anikó Hatoss

All English Accents Matter
In Pursuit of Accent Equity, Diversity, and Inclusion
Pierre Wilbert Orelus

For more information about this series, please visit www.routledge.com/Routledge-Studies-in-Sociolinguistics/book-series/RSSL

All English Accents Matter
In Pursuit of Accent Equity, Diversity, and Inclusion

Pierre Wilbert Orelus

NEW YORK AND LONDON

First published 2023
by Routledge
605 Third Avenue, New York, NY 10158

and by Routledge
4 Park Square, Milton Park, Abingdon, Oxon, OX14 4RN

Routledge is an imprint of the Taylor & Francis Group, an informa business

© 2023 Taylor & Francis

The right of Pierre Wilbert Orelus to be identified as author of this work has been asserted in accordance with sections 77 and 78 of the Copyright, Designs and Patents Act 1988.

All rights reserved. No part of this book may be reprinted or reproduced or utilised in any form or by any electronic, mechanical, or other means, now known or hereafter invented, including photocopying and recording, or in any information storage or retrieval system, without permission in writing from the publishers.

Trademark notice: Product or corporate names may be trademarks or registered trademarks and are used only for identification and explanation without intent to infringe.

Library of Congress Cataloging-in-Publication Data
Names: Orelus, Pierre W., author.
Title: All English accents matter : in pursuit of accent equity, diversity, and inclusion / Pierre Wilbert Orelus.
Description: New York, NY : Routledge, 2023. | Series: Routledge studies in sociolinguistics | Includes bibliographical references and index.
Identifiers: LCCN 2022049201 | Subjects: LCSH: English language—Social aspects. | English language—Pronunciation by foreign speakers. | Discrimination in language. | Speech and social status.
Classification: LCC PE1074.75 .O74 2023 | DDC 306.442/21—dc23/eng/20230104
LC record available at https://lccn.loc.gov/2022049201

ISBN: 978-0-415-72270-4 (hbk)
ISBN: 978-1-032-46091-8 (pbk)
ISBN: 978-1-315-85813-5 (ebk)

DOI: 10.4324/9781315858135

Typeset in Times New Roman
by Apex CoVantage, LLC

To bilingual and multilingual students, including immigrant and international students, whom I have had the opportunity to teach and learn from over the last two decades or more. The painful experiences with accent discrimination YOU shared with me inspired me to embark on the case study leading to the materialization of this book. Thank you!

Contents

	Foreword	viii
	JOHN BAUGH	
1	The Coloniality of Western Language Hegemony	1
2	All English Accents Matter	23
3	Affirming Accent Variation	40
4	Linguistic and Racial Inequities in Higher Education: *The Subaltern Speak Out*	54
5	In Pursuit of Linguistic Equity, Diversity, and Inclusion	69
6	Exposing the Effects of Linguoelitism on Linguistic Minorities	74
	Appendix	85
	Index	110

Foreword

Linguists have grappled with a conceptual paradox since the inception of the field; from a purely theoretical perspective, all languages are created equal, but history has confirmed that some languages, or dialects, are more highly valued than others. Another anomaly grows from the myriad of unpredictable quirks that influence linguistic evolution. For example, many words have more than one meaning, and meanings are intricately linked to the contexts in which they are used. If someone is said to be *discriminating*, does that refer to the fact that they are a discerning connoisseur, or does that imply that they engage in unfair prejudicial behavior? Both interpretations are viable, and, depending upon the context in which a *discriminating* person is defined, their discriminatory behavior may either be laudable or shameful.

Language, as embodied through different modes of speaking, often serves as a surrogate for other social forms of demarcation, such as race, gender, sexual orientation, or class. Readers of this book will discover many forms of linguistic discrimination that are contained within a series of case studies that offer multilingual and multinational perspectives on the topic. Particular attention is given to some of the harmful consequences of accent discrimination in educational contexts.

The content of this book will be informative to a wide audience, because your opinions about language are unique to the linguistic circumstances you know best. Therein lies one of the hidden virtues of this book, because the case studies that reveal instances of linguistic discrimination, while highly personal and idiosyncratic, will be (un)familiar to different readers, and therefore educative in different ways. Those who have been raised in well-educated families that emphasize the importance of "proper" language usage are likely to interpret each case study differently from readers who have learned English as a secondary language.

Your educational exposure and subsequent opportunities, or lack thereof, will also serve to reinforce or broaden your views and opinions regarding matters of linguistic diversity, and how best to address them in societies where differential access to wealth, political power, and professional opportunities prevail. Toward this end, readers will be introduced to the concept of *linguoelitism*, which is presented in ways that illustrate many of the negative consequences of misplaced impressions of linguistic superiority, along with innovative ideas about how best to overcome linguistic discrimination that frequently results from a combination of residential, educational, occupational, and linguistic insularity.

Pierre Wilbert Orelus begins with self-reflective insights derived from his own childhood in Haiti. He then takes the reader on a journey through the lives of people who have fallen prey to various forms of linguistic discrimination first-hand, throughout the world. These highly personal portrayals, case studies all, do more that expose the reader to the travails that result from linguistic prejudice; they set the stage for challenging "accentism" while deftly revealing the combination of historical and social circumstances that frequently give rise to linguistic domination or subordination.

This book culminates with keen insights regarding the incontrovertible relationship between accent discrimination and political power, echoing Sam Weinreich's edict that a standard language is defined by those who control military might. Illustrations of well-known public figures who speak with strong accents, while having achieved success, wealth, and public acclaim, are presented in stark contrast to others whose language belies their race, or gender, or sexual orientation. This book does more than expose this discriminatory legacy, it strives to alert us to the negative consequences of misplaced linguistic elitism and its divisive ramifications.

Pierre Wilbert Orelus provides us with harsh truths that demand attention, particularly because the need to promote greater social harmony within nation states and internationally has never been greater than at this point in time. He sounds alarms that have, for far too long, gone unnoticed; and, in so doing, he seeks to enlist you—the reader—in his quest to promote linguistic equality throughout the world.

John Baugh
Margaret Bush Wilson Professor in Arts and Sciences
Washington University in St. Louis
Professor Emeritus of Education and Linguistics
Stanford University

1 The Coloniality of Western Language Hegemony

One's interest in, or passion for, any subject matter usually stems from one's existential experiences. My interest in accent and language issues, which this book explores, is fundamentally linked to my early schooling experiences in a colonized land, Haiti. It is worth situating such a claim in its proper context. I grew up speaking two languages, Creole and French, intermingling and influencing each other, yet holding uneven sociolinguistic status.

There was, and still is, an asymmetrical power relation between these two languages. In Haiti, where I was born and raised, standard French was, and is still, the much-preferred language of the elite, while Creole was, and still is, the language working-class people use at home, in their neighborhood, and in schools to interact with one another. By contrast, those from middle- to upper-middle class backgrounds usually use French for the same or similar purposes (Degraff, 2018, 2019; Orelus, 2020).

My early experiences living in a rural area, and later in an overcrowded city, Port-au-Prince, helped me realize that there were, and there are still, regional accent differences in the way Haitians speak Creole. While classmates from northern areas like Cape Haitian took pride in saying that their Creole was original, those from Port-au-Prince challenged them by arguing that their Creole was French-based and, therefore, better–a linguistic divide that stems from what Degraff (2003) calls "Creole exceptionalism". This form of exceptionalism is linked to the French colonial legacy, and has created unequal linguistic power relations among Haitians.

My early schooling experiences enabled me to understand the linguistic gap between Creole, the language spoken by the Haitian masses, and French, the language of the colonizer, mainly spoken by the Haitian elite and the middle class. This linguistic divide stemming from the French colonial legacy has linguistically and academically affected disenfranchised Haitians in particular and all Haitian students generally. Haitians from

DOI: 10.4324/9781315858135-1

working-class families were, and are still, looked down upon because of their regional, working-class accent.

I was, for example, often told, and continue to be told, that I speak "good" French, expecting me to take it as a form of a compliment. I felt, and still feel, otherwise, as I knew it was a form of accentism. A French accent that is close to a Parisian type of accent, which Haitian students, particularly those of the petit bourgeois class, have been emulating, is considered a good accent. While the majority of poor working-class students were, and still are, subjected to discrimination in schools and society at large because of their regional accents and perceived inability to speak "proper" French, middle- and upper-middle-class students were, and are, continuously praised, for their fluency in the French language as well as their "good" accent (Orelus, 2020).

Throughout my K-12 school years, I was exposed to, and witnessed, many forms of accent discrimination, most of which were class-based. My early formal schooling experience taught me about unequal power relations between standard accents and oppressed ones. Specifically, such experiences made me realize that there was, and there is still, linguistic inequity between Creole, my mother tongue, and French, the dominant language that I learned in schools. Such linguistic inequity stems from the legacy of colonization during which French was imposed on the slaves imported from Africa (Degraff, 2001, 2018, 2019; James, 1989). Awareness of this historical fact has enabled me to understand the asymmetrical power relations between languages. In school, I was formally educated in French, and, both at home and in my neighborhood, I used, and continue to use, Creole to interact with my parents, relatives, neighbors, and close friends. I witnessed accent discrimination to which working class Haitian citizens, particularly those living in rural areas, were, and continue to be, subjected.

This type of linguistic divide has profoundly and historically shaped the structure of school systems of many countries, including that of Haiti. For example, standard French, the language that has been imposed on Haitians since colonial time, tends to be valued and appreciated more than Haitian Creole, the maternal language of most Haitians. Standard French is associated with higher social class status than Creole, and seen as a ticket to upward socioeconomic and political mobility. Creole, by contrast, is perceived and treated as a second-class type of language, that is, some sort of a dialect, which is routinely looked down upon.

As a result of this divide, those who master standard French are often assumed to be of higher intelligence than those who do not, and tend to do be admired generally (Orelus et al., 2014). Moreover, fluent standard French speakers in Haiti tend to have an easier time securing employment at professional levels. Finally, Haitians who speak standard French usually receive formal education, and have the opportunity to attend well-resourced schools. They tend to be middle and upper middle class, and they do not experience the linguistic mismatch between home and school that poor, working-class Haitian students experience, for their home environment is not so different from that of the elite schools they attend (Orelus et al., 2014).

As shown above, my interest in accent and language issues stems from the junction of my early personal and academic experiences. Such experiences would later help me better understand the similarity between standard French, the dominant language in Haiti, and standard English, the hegemonic language in the United States. My passion for the study of accent in particular would later be heightened by an inspirational encounter with an influential sociolinguistics professor, originally from Cape Verde, while I was a graduate student at University of Massachusetts, Boston. Specifically, in his sociolinguistics seminar, he often shared with us moving personal stories regarding accent discrimination he experienced as a bilingual student and later as a university professor.

The level of depth and enthusiasm he demonstrated while talking about the politics of language and accent inspired me to develop a deep interest in the field of sociolinguistics. he introduced us to a wide range of literature connected to bilingual education, multilingualism, as well as the hegemony of standard English. He critically discussed challenges facing linguistically and culturally diverse student populations, particularly bilingual and multilingual students, and I have grown to become keenly aware of, and appreciate, linguistic and cultural diversity as a result of this experience.

Upon completing my master's degree in applied linguistics, I was offered a teaching position at a high school located in one of the most racially and economically segregated American neighborhoods, Dorchester, in Boston, Massachusetts. Teaching students from all walks of life, including students born in the United States but for whom English is their second language, I learned valuable teaching and life lessons that contributed to my becoming a compassionate and dedicated educator. For example, I learned first-hand that, contrary to America's basic promises of equity and equal access to a quality education, immigrant bilingual students routinely experienced language and accent discrimination, in addition to racial and socio-economic inequalities.

I begin this introduction drawing from narratives grounded in both my personal and academic experiences to delineate where my passion for accent and language issues originates, and to also explain the underlying reasons for writing this book. The sections that follow explore in depth the colonial roots of the domination of western languages, such as English and French, and standard accent on others and their implications for linguistically minoritized people speaking these languages with a distinct accent.

Affirming Language and Accent Diversity: No to Linguistic Apartheid!

Language is perhaps the most common issue that surfaces in debates revolving around school reforms, human rights, human relations, and development, as well as the history of colonialism, among other things. It plays a vital role in virtually everything we are involved in. Besides shaping our identity and being a medium whereby we remain connected to our community and express our view of the world, language has historically been utilized as a tool of domination and conquest. The politics of language has been at the center of the scholarly work of linguists, sociolinguists, critical theorists, and educators (Darder, 1991; Gee, 2014; Macedo et al., 2003; Orelus et al., 2014; Pennycook, 2017).

In light of this work, the rest of this chapter examines the "linguistic apartheid" that occurred during the colonial era and continues to happen in the United States with the "English-only" movement. By linguistic apartheid I mean the subjugation of certain languages by dominant European and American groups who have, throughout history, tried to impose hegemonic languages, such as English, French, and Portuguese, on colonized and marginalized groups at the expense of the native languages of these groups. To illuminate how this form of apartheid has occurred, this book begins by providing a historical overview of the way many languages and accents labeled as inferior have been attacked and pushed to the margins, discriminating against those who speak them. It goes on to analyze the effect such actions have had on the culture, the identity, the learning process, and the subjective and material conditions of linguistically diverse groups. The book ends by proposing alternative ways to counter language and standard-accent hegemony that minority groups, including bilingual students and English-language learners, have faced in schools and in society at large.

Examining Linguistic Apartheid in American Schools and Society

Historically, minority languages have been attacked and relegated to an inferior status through the mechanism of colonization and slavery and, recently, with the English-only movement in the United States (Macedo et al., 2003; Phillipson, 2010; Orelus, 2007). Consequently, people who by accident of birth happen to speak these languages have been marginalized, oppressed, and discriminated against in schools and society at large. For example, in the United States, Native American children, forcibly placed in reservations, were often reprimanded in government schools for speaking native languages perceived by their teachers as uncivilized (Spring, 2019). Likewise, Aboriginal children in Australia were compulsorily taken from their families and placed in boarding schools where they were prohibited from speaking their native tongue, and their names were changed to Anglo names (Olsen, 2003; Phillipson, 2013).

Similarly, in South America, particularly in Peru, the Spaniards attempted unsuccessfully to completely wipe out the native language of the Andeans, Quechua (Pratt, 1999). Texts written in Quechua by the Indigenous Andeans took centuries before they were finally published. A 1,200-page letter written by an Indigenous Andean, Felipe Guaman de Ayala, is a case in point. Written in 1613 and found by a Peruvian, Richard Pietschmann, Ayala's letter was not made available to the general public until 1912 (Pratt, 1999). Pratt maintains, "Quechua was not thought of as a written language in 1908, nor Andean culture as a literate culture" (p. 584).

Likewise, in his seminal book, *How Europe Underdeveloped Africa*, Walter Rodney (1972) documents how and to what extent European colonizers imposed their languages on African children in order to maintain their linguistic, political, and socio-economic domination. According to Rodney, to achieve this goal, the European colonizers hired colonial submissive teachers to teach European culture and history to African students in kindergarten and primary schools. Through this colonial form of schooling, African students were taught to value and embrace the language and culture of their colonizers at the expense of their own. Rodney states:

> Schools of kindergarten and primary level for Africans in Portuguese colonies were nothing but agencies for the spread of the Portuguese language. Most schools were controlled by the Catholic Church, as a reflection of the unity of church and state in fascist Portugal. In the little-known Spanish colony of Guinea (Rio Muni), the small amount of education given to Africans was based on eliminating the use of local languages by the pupils and on instilling in their hearts the holy fear of God.
>
> (p. 249)

African students were taught to simply become ignorant of their own languages, culture, history, and geography, which, according to Rodney, colonial teachers never talked about in class. While colonized students learned in school about the "Alps and the river Rhine", they were denied vital information about the "Atlas Mountains of North Africa or the river Zambezi" (Rodney, p. 247). Rodney further argues that as early as in kindergarten, the colonized African students knew more about Napoleon Bonaparte, who reestablished slavery in Guadeloupe and attempted unsuccessfully to do the

6 *The Coloniality of Western Language Hegemony*

same in Haiti, than their own ancestors. This form of oppression Indigenous and colonized people suffered and continue to endure has impacted them linguistically, culturally, educationally, and psychologically (Smith, 2019; Wane, 2006). As Wane (2006) observes:

> The use of a foreign language as a medium of education makes a child foreign within her or his own culture, environment, etc. This creates a colonial alienation. What is worse, the neo-colonized subject is made to see the world and where she or he stands in it as seen and defined by or reflected in the culture of the language of imposition. This is made worse when the neo-colonized subject is exposed to images of her or his world mirrored in the written language of her or his colonizer, where the natives' language, cultures, history, or people are associated with low status, slow intelligence, and barbarism.
>
> (Wane in Sefa & Kempf, 2006, p. 100)

What can be inferred from the argument above is that the goal of the European colonizers was to ensure that the colonized African students did not have a good command of their languages or a sound understanding of their culture and history. They were forced to learn the French, Portuguese, and English languages and cultures, so that they could quickly assimilate into the European culture. Consequently, many may have grown to appreciate European languages and culture much more than their own.

In his book *Deculturalization and the Struggle for Equality*, Joel Spring (2019) maintains that through schooling Indigenous students were taught that their language, culture, and Indigenous knowledge were inferior, barbarous, uncivilized, and therefore worthless in comparison to the European-based culture and knowledge they received in schools. Similarly, in *Linguistic Imperialism Continued*, Robert Phillipson (2013) astutely documents how European countries, particularly the U.K., and the United States have continued to impose English on the world as the lingua franca, that is, *the* language that people around the globe should use to communicate—whether it be for personal, professional, or business purposes–and study, at the expense of Indigenous and native languages of billions of people, including bilingual students. Phillipson warns, "When analyzing English Worldwide the crux of the matter is whose interests English serves, and whose interests scholarship on English serves" (p. 27).

The linguistic and cultural oppression that Native American children in the U.S., Aboriginal children in Australia, the Tainos in the Caribbean, colonized Africans, and other marginalized groups experienced and continue to experience can be best described by what Paulo Freire (1920) calls "cultural invasion".

Gandhi (2009), Nyerere (1968), and Thiong'o (1986), among many others, understood the educational implications of the cultural invasion eloquently articulated by Freire. Throughout their political and academic careers, they resisted colonial linguistic and cultural influences on the school system of their countries, India, Tanzania, and Kenya respectively. For example, Gandhi (1997) advocated for an educational system that met the linguistic needs and reflected the cultural traditions, beliefs, and aspirations of the Indian people. While Gandhi did not object to the idea that students should learn the English language, he argued that it should not be done at the expense of Indian Indigenous language(s), which needed to be valued and instituted in schools. Gandhi as disheartened by and therefore spoke against the dominance of English throughout public and private institutions in Indian society.

One's native language should never be sacrificed, regardless of the circumstances, for it is through that language that one can better learn in school and express one's aspirations and view of the world. Simply stated, one's native language is the language through which one can truly feel at ease in the world. Unfortunately, linguistic apartheid stemming from European and American linguistic domination has led to the marginalization of many languages and people around the world.

Like Gandhi (1997), Nyerere (1968) and Thiong'o (1986) challenged the educational system in Tanzania and Kenya respectively. Colonial school systems are designed to prepare students to serve the interest of the colonizers. Nyerere (1968) and Thiong'o (1986) both advocated for an educational system that would value and embrace the native local languages and culture of Tanzanians and Kenyans and prepare them to serve the interest of their country. Nyerere states, "The education provided by Tanzania for the students of Tanzania must serve the purposes of Tanzania. It must encourage the growth of the socialist values we aspire to" (p. 32). Similarly, Thiong'o, who was jailed and beaten for daring to speak against British colonialism that negated local languages and cultural practices of Kenyan students and families, maintains:

> In schools and universities our Kenyan languages—that is the languages of the many nationalities which make up Kenya—were associated with negative qualities of backwardness, underdevelopment, humiliation, and punishment. We who went through that school system

were meant to graduate with a hatred of the people and the culture and the values of the language of our daily humiliation and punishment. I do not want to see Kenyan children growing up in that imperialist imposed tradition of contempt for the tools of communication developed by their communities and their history. I want them to transcend colonial alienation.

(p. 28)

What Thiong'o describes above is still happening to people in Caribbean, African, and Latin American countries that are officially independent but continue to experience a renewed form of linguistic, educational, socioeconomic, and political colonialism. For instance, as analyzed in the concluding chapter, people in formerly colonized countries like Haiti are still under the subjugation of French-language hegemony (Orelus, 2020). The educated, upper-middle-class Haitians, especially those who were educated in France, take pride in speaking only French to interact with friends, family, and colleagues., those who use Creole to communicate their thoughts, aspirations, and feelings in the public sphere are sometimes regarded as uneducated and looked down upon (Orelus, 2020).

In *Black Skin White Mask*, Fanon (2008) uses the example of middle-class people in his native Martinique to illustrate a similar form of linguistic colonial practice. Fanon states, "The middle class in the Antilles never speak Creole except to their servants. In school the children of Martinique are taught to scorn the dialect. One avoids Creolisms. Some families completely forbid the use of Creole, and mothers ridicule their children for speaking it" (p. 20).

The colonial practices described above are not occurring only in Caribbean countries. They have been recurring in western school systems and societies, including in the U.S., especially with the English-only movement, to which I turn next.

The English-only Movement: A Neocolonial Form of Linguistic Domination

Despite the widespread rhetoric that the U.S. is a melting pot, a multilingual and democratic country, minority languages and so-called foreign accents have been stigmatized and relegated to an inferior position (Baugh, 2018). Proponents of the English-only movement have wanted minority groups to embrace and speak only English at the expense of their native tongues. Consequently, students who have used their human agency to resist this form of linguistic domination by sticking to their cultural heritage and mother tongue in various settings, such as in school and at work, have been severely castigated. In her classic study on language discrimination in schools conducted with Latino students, Villegas (1988) reported that some White middle-class teachers prohibited Latino students from speaking Spanish in class. Villegas stated that these teachers felt that speaking Spanish in school was a way of persisting in being foreign. She went on to say that, although 90% of the students were U.S. citizens, their teachers treated them as outsiders because they persisted in speaking Spanish.

Gloria Anzaldua's (1990) experience with a xenophobic Anglo teacher who forbade her from speaking Spanish in class exemplifies what Villegas reported in her study. Anzaldua recounts:

> I remember being caught speaking Spanish at recess—that was good for three licks on the knuckles with a sharp ruler. I remember being sent to the corner of the classroom for "talking back" to the Anglo teacher when all I was trying to do was tell her how to pronounce my name. "If you want to be American, speak 'American.' If you don't like it, go back to Mexico where you belong".
>
> (p. 203)

Anzaldua's experience with the Anglo teacher clearly illustrates how those who believe in and embrace the English-only movement have committed "symbolic violence" (Bourdieu, 1999) against marginalized groups by trying to silence their voices. It also shows the struggle of minority students, including bilingual students and English-language learners, whose home discourse and culture often do not fit into the mainstream discourse and culture (Darder, 1991; Nieto, 2009). Moreover, her experience illustrates that language is not simply about uttering words but is intrinsically linked to ideology, culture, and power relations (Darder, 1991).

Finally, the linguistic discrimination that Anzaldua faced in school puts into question the belief that the United States is a free and democratic country. In a country that has been called democratic and free, people should not be threatened and punished for speaking their native tongues and accents. Prohibiting someone from speaking their language suggests that one is free in the land of the free as long as one does not speak Spanish, Creole, or other subjugated languages. Taking this analysis a step further, I argue that prohibiting people from speaking their native languages is a way to promote English as the "lingua franca" (Phillipson, 1992). This type of linguistic assault against minority languages appears to have as its objective to put English into a class of its own. This, as a consequence, might "reinforce the dominant ideology, which presupposes that English is the most eligible language for virtually all significant purposes" (p. 42).

Although Anzaldua's experience with her Anglo teacher happened over two decades ago, it is still relevant, for minority students continue to experience linguistic discrimination in schools. An attack against minority native languages is not a simple matter. As Darder (1991) argues, "negating the native language and its potential benefits in the development of the student's voice constitutes a form of psychological violence and functions to perpetuate social control over subordinate language groups through various linguistic forms of cultural invasion" (p. 38).

Negating the native languages of marginalized groups is informed by the ideological and political agenda of dominant groups who have tried to impose English, for example, as *the* standard language, as if the languages these groups speak are inferior. Unveiling the fallacy about and the linguistic injustice embedded in the English-only movement, Freire and Macedo (1987) maintain:

> The English only movement in the United States . . . points to a xenophobic culture that blindly negates the pluralistic nature of U.S. society and falsifies the empirical evidence in support of bilingual education, as has been amply documented. These educators, including the present secretary of Education, William Bennet, fail to understand that it is through multiple discourses that students generate meaning in their everyday social context.
>
> (p. 154)

The dominant class is determined to use English as the lingua franca to maintain the status quo, Freire and Macedo argue (Phillipson, 1992), revealing the hidden ideological battle over which language is superior or inferior. The social and historical construction of English as a "superior language" consequently leads to the marginalization of other languages. It seems that the English-only movement has been used as an ideological tool to normalize linguistic discrimination against minority groups.

One of the arguments that proponents of the English-only movement, such as the California businessman Ron Unz, have articulated for imposing English on linguistically and culturally diverse groups is that speaking one language will unify the nation and that bilingual education is detrimental to the learning of minority students, particularly bilingual students. Taken at face value, this argument might convince one to believe that bilingual students would be better off being placed in mainstream classrooms where English is the only language of instruction, and that unity among people can be achieved only through one dominant, officially recognized and established language, like English, but not through a plurality and diversity of languages. Hirsch, for example, believes that unity among culturally and linguistically diverse groups can be achieved only through what he called "common culture".

With regard to the achievement gap existing between underprivileged and privileged students, Hirsh argues that this gap stems from the student's lack of a particular and prescribed set of cultural knowledge, which, according to him, can be learned through direct instruction. However, Kamberelis and Dimitriadis (2005) note that, "The cultural knowledge that Hirsh has in mind is presumed to be 'common culture' and not elite culture, even though it derives primarily from canonical works within a White, European-American, middle-upper-class, heterosexist tradition" (p. 30).

What Hirsch fails to understand is that individuals do not give up their native tongue even when they are forced to embrace the so-called common culture. The reason is that one's language shapes one's identity and life. Thus, attacking one's language is a direct attack on one's culture and identity. As Anzaldua (1990) puts it:

> If you want to really hurt me, talk badly about my language. Ethnic identity is twin skin to linguistic identity—I am my language. Until I can take pride in my language, I cannot take pride in myself. Until I can accept as legitimate Chicano Texas Spanish, Tex-Mex and all the other languages I speak, I cannot accept the legitimacy of myself.
> (p. 473)

Anzaldua's stance regarding/toward her language and identity clearly indicates that language "plays a major role in the construction of human subjectivities and reflects their life histories and lived experiences" (Freire and Macedo, 1987, p. 56). Most importantly, it illustrates that, "Like desire, language disrupts, refuses to be contained within boundaries. It speaks itself against our will, in words and thoughts that intrude, even violate the most private spaces of mind and body" (hooks, 1994, p. 66). Given the persistent linguistic discrimination occurring in schools and society at large, the question then becomes, what needs to be done to overturn linguistic apartheid that continues to impact the learning and the minds of students? The next section attempts to shed light on this question.

Resisting Linguistic Domination

Overcoming linguistic apartheid as well as other forms of oppression that marginalized groups have faced would require them to engage in cultural resistance (Cabral, 1973) against their oppressor and the decolonization of their minds (Thiong'o, 1986), among other things. How should this be done? There is no single, fixed answer to this question. A plausible answer must be sought through dialoguing with one another and critically reflecting on linguistic, political, and social problems that the legacy of colonialism has caused. The challenge, however, is that it is not only the mind of marginalized peoples that need to be decolonized but also the imposed languages of the colonizers that they daily use. As Salman Rushdie (1982) points out: "The language, like so much else in the colonies, needs to be decolonized, to be remade in other images, if those of us who use it from positions outside Anglo-Saxon culture are to be more than artistic Uncle Toms" (Rushdie cited in McLeod, 2001, p. 67). Along the same lines, McLeod (2001) proposes that, "in order to challenge the colonial order of things, some of us may need to re-examine our received assumptions of what we have been taught as 'natural' or 'true'" (p. 54).

Achieving what Rushdie and McLeod suggest would require what Freire (2020) called "*conscientizao*", that is, critical consciousness of one's linguistic, socio-economic, and political realities. Such consciousness is necessary to deconstruct, challenge, and resist linguistic domination alongside other forms of oppression perpetuated through teachers' biases and ideology, and the western colonial values embedded in canonical texts many teachers are expected to use in schools. To put it simply, linguistic and cultural domination get reproduced through the way teachers use and engage students in these texts.

Depending on how teachers approach and analyze canonical texts, including textbooks, with their students, their teaching practices can empower the latter to reproduce and/or contest cultural values embedded in those texts. Canagarajah (1993), for example, recounts his experience using western imported textbooks to teach English to 22 students coming from poorly educated rural families in Sri Lanka, whose primary language is Tamil. The key textbook selected for the freshman English course was American Kernel Lessons.

According to Canagarajah (1993), textbooks used in the school were donated by Western cultural agencies. Students enrolled in the English course were required to pass a mandatory English placement test in order to be admitted to university. Canagarajah reported that the content of these textbooks reflected the cultural, linguistic, and social class realities of White middle-class Americans to which his Sri Lankan students could not relate. However, Canagarajah found ways to help students develop a counter-discourse to strategically resist these western hegemonic texts. Canagarajah explains his students' strategic approach and resistance to these texts in the following terms:

> Through these counter-discourses, students could be detaching themselves from the discourses inscribed in the textbook and preserving

themselves from ideological reproduction. Furthermore, students are able to construct for themselves more favorable subjectivities and identities through their counterdiscourses. While the discourses of the textbook put students at a disadvantage, making them appear alien, incompetent, inferior and powerless, students' own discourses provide them confidence, familiarity, respectability and greater power in their social milieu.

(p. 151)

Canagarajah illuminates how teachers can help students develop a language of critique to unveil hidden ideology embedded in texts. Acknowledging the strong presence and important role of ideology in language issues, Fairclough (1997) maintains that "a critical analysis of language is crucial for social change" (p. 89). In the same vein, Dei and Kempf (2006) notes:

Language is a powerful tool for decolonization. The power to name issues for what they are demonstrates an ability to use language as resistance, and to claim cultural and political capital that is necessary to challenge domination. The power of anti-colonial thinking lies in its ability to name the domination and imposition of colonial relations. Language can be used to challenge the negations, omissions, and devaluations of a peoples' social reality, experience, and history.

(p. 11)

Dei and Kempf (2006) brilliantly captures the important use of language in both production and distribution of power between marginalized and dominant groups. Marginalized groups have always had to fight against the linguistic and cultural domination of the ruling class. However, despite their resistance, marginalized groups in the U.S. have experienced some losses. For example, bilingual programs in the U.S., which have allowed linguistically and culturally diverse students to maintain and use their first language to learn and succeed in school, have been closed in many states, such as California, Arizona, and Massachusetts. Consequently, school systems in these states are experiencing a shortage of certified and properly trained bilingual teachers to work with bilingual students and English-language learners (Crawford, 2008). The elimination of the bilingual programs in these states and others is one of the negative consequences of the English-only movement.

To continue to counter this movement, along with other forms of linguistic and cultural domination in schools and beyond, it is critically important that educators help the public develop critical and political consciousness about the "hegemony of the English" (Macedo et al., 2003). This consciousness would help subaltern groups better understand (1) that being forced to speak the so-called language of opportunity, for example, English, at the expense of their first languages is convincing evidence of the dominant class's linguistic domination strategies; (2) that by being forced to embrace the language of the dominant class, they would automatically embrace values, beliefs, and norms embedded in that language; and (3) that once these cultural elements are ingrained in their linguistic repertoire and consciousness, it then would be easier for the dominant class to manipulate and control their minds.

Fanon (2020) understood the ideological and cultural significance of possessing a language when he warned us: "A man who has a language consequently possesses the world expressed and implied by that language" (p. 18). Situating Fanon's argument in the U.S. context, it can be argued that once minority students, through ideological manipulation, are convinced to value and embrace the English language along with the American or British standard accent at the expense of their own, the cultural world of their oppressor to a great extent will become theirs. As Thiong'o states, "Language carries culture, and culture carries, particularly through orature and literature, the entire body of values by which we come to perceive ourselves and our place in the world" (p. 16).

To build on Thiong'o's argument, it is worth referring here to the work of Amilcar Cabral (1973), particularly his stance on culture. The Guinean and Cape Verdean leader, who fought rigorously against the Portuguese colonizers' cultural invasion in Cape Verde and Guinea Bissau, strongly urged people to defend their culture. Cabral dedicated most of his militant, political, and scholarly life to defending the culture of his country, both nationally and internationally, against foreign cultural invasion. In his classic book *Return to the Source*, Cabral strongly encourages us to strive to preserve our culture from the colonial and imperial influence of the West. Cabral used culture as a tool of resistance to foreign subjugation of colonized lands, such as Cape Verde and Guinea Bissau. He did not merely acknowledge the vital role of culture in the liberation movement. He also advocated for its full integration in the historical and political life of these colonized societies at the time. He did so because he understood that imperialist and colonial domination of colonized subjects also entails the cultural domination of the latter. Thus, Cabral strove to help his people be aware of the importance of using their cultural resources and values as a counter-weapon in their fight against imperial and colonial powers. Cabral (1973) maintains:

> It is understood that imperialist domination, by denying the historical development of the dominated people, necessarily also denies their

cultural development. It is also understood why imperialist domination, like all other foreign domination, for its own security, requires cultural oppression and the attempt at direct or indirect liquidation of the essential elements of the culture of the dominated people.

(p. 55)

Drawing on Cabral's view on the political and historical importance of culture, I contend that culture and language are vital tools that colonizers and neo-colonizers should never be allowed to dominate, especially when a people engage in the struggle for self-affirmation, self-determination, and linguistic liberation. The reason is that if colonized or minority people's language and accents and culture are constantly under attack, this will affect their self-esteem and their spirit of resistance. Defense and preservation of one's language is key to one's cultural identity. It is equally important for students, teachers, parents, and the general public to be aware of standard accent hegemony that further perpetuates linguistic apartheid in schools and society at large. Drawing from case studies conducted over the course of five years, this book examines such hegemony, which needs to be challenged and exposed, for it silences the diverse types of accents and languages of linguistic minorities.

Exposing Standard Accent Hegemony

There are privileges associated with standard accents, as we live in a society where such accents are highly valued. Generally, those who speak in the standard English accent, for instance, are seen through a positive lens linguistically; they are often put in more privileged positions in society than those whose native language and accent are stigmatized (Baugh, 2018; Cummins, 2016; Lippi-Green, 2012; Phillipson, 1992). Historically, linguistically dominant groups have had an easier time navigating through the system to achieve higher academic, professional, and political goals than those whose accents are not appreciated or valued in mainstream society (Lippi-Green, 2012; Marvasti, 2005; Matsuda, 1991). Indeed, people who speak with a perceivable non-dominant accent frequently often face accent discrimination, like linguistic profiling, in schools, at work, and in housing and employment searches (Baugh, 2000, 2018; Gluszek and Dovidio, 2010).

Depending on where one's accent originates, one may be subject to insidious forms of accent discrimination. For example, ethnic and linguistic minorities, including immigrant bilingual students, are routinely subjected to accent discrimination because of their non-standard accent (Baugh, 2018; Cummins, 2016; Garcia and Kleifgen, 2018; Macedo, 2019; Nieto and

Bode, 2018). In higher education, bilingual college and university professors and students, whose English accents differ from the alleged standard American accent, often experience accent discrimination in spite of their academic and professional achievements (Macedo, 2019; Torres, 2004).

As an example, Myriam Torres (2004), a university professor born and raised in Colombia, talks about the way in which she faces linguistic discrimination and xenophobia because of her distinct English accent. Torres (2004) claims that she often has to challenge those who have ill-perceived and poorly treated her because of her accent. In a powerful essay, *To the Margins and Back: The High Cost of Being Latina in "America"*, she narrates:

> Very often I have to deal with people's suspicious attitudes. Hence, the basic civil rights under which an individual is innocent until the contrary is proved do not work in my case. I often find myself in situations in which I am prejudged negatively and therefore have to prove that people are wrong in their assumptions about me. It is evident to me that my physical characteristics of Latina and my Spanish accent in English are enough to unleash their negative assumptions about Latinos and immigrants. Proving to people that their prejudgments about abilities, expertise, and potential are inappropriate and unfair is a very difficult task to carry out due to the prejudgments themselves. I am given very few opportunities to do so.
>
> (p. 130)

As her narrative suggests, because of her non-dominant English accent, Torres (2004) often has to prove to people that she is intellectually capable in order to get the respect that she deserves–something her White, middle-class, monolingual colleagues might not have to do. It is ironic American pundits have called United States a democratic country and have tried to portray it as a role model for the world, while people who speak in a different English accent continue to be discriminated against. Isn't it hypocritical to call a country democratic where certain groups have been linguistically stereotyped and discriminated against for speaking in a different English accent? Targeting people because of their accent contradicts the very idea that this country is democratic. We must, therefore, ask: are we truly living in a democratic country? If so, for whom has this country been a democratic country? The noble idea of democracy needs to be a reality not only for those who happen to speak English or French with "the right accent", but also for those who speak it with various accents and from diverse linguistic and ethnic backgrounds.

Accent has added varied layers to the identity of diverse linguistic groups, particularly bilingual and multilingual students (Cummins, 2016, 2017; García and Lin, 2017). When people immigrate from a country to another, they bring their linguistic repertoire, which expands over time; their accent, which is part of this repertoire, evolves over time through interaction with other accents spoken by people from other linguistic and cultural backgrounds. Africans, for example, who were captured and forcibly transported to the Americas only to be enslaved, spoke in various accents and languages. Through interaction with other Africans and later slaves, their native languages and accents evolved, borrowing words from other languages and accents (Baugh, 2018; Gilyard, 2011).

The factors identified and analyzed earlier influence how minoritized accents are perceived and treated in society in comparison to others. Accent inequity affects bilingual linguistic minority groups in multi-dimensional ways; it intersects with other systemic forms of oppression, including xenophobia, racism, and classism. As a result, linguistic minorities have been discriminated against not only because of their noticeably accented English, for example, but also because of their ethnicity, race, and nationality, regardless of their American citizenship, complicating the whole notion of citizenship. They are often not protected under the basic right to speak their native language that their White European and American counterparts enjoy as citizens. Nieto (2002) asks,

> Is one an American by the mere fact of being born here? Can one be born elsewhere and still be an American? How many generations does it take? Do we belong here and there, in neither place, or in both? Does being an American have to erase or diminish automatically our accents, our values, our hues and textures? Where does our language, which sometimes is unacceptable both in our communities of origin and in the larger society, fit in? Do we have to 'trade in' our identity, much as we would an old car, to acquire the shiny new image of American?
>
> (p. 105)

Nieto's questions suggest that accent, native language, and country-of-origin issues should challenge one to rethink and question the notion of citizenship, as linguistic minorities have often been discriminated against because of these factors. They often determine who has been actually treated with dignity, civility, and inclusivity in this country, and who has not. U.S. citizens, including naturalized immigrants, have been subjected to stigma and stereotypes because their English accents are often associated with their ethnicity and country of origin.

I argue that everyone speaks with an accent, whether it be called standard, foreign, or heavy. However, because of unequal power relations among speakers, certain groups have been placed in more favorable linguistic positions than others, such as African Americans who have been targeted and discriminated against for speaking Ebonics (Baugh, 2000, 2018; Labov, 2011). Similarly, as some case studies show, U.S.-born Latinx, who grew up speaking English as their native language, have been discriminated against because of their accent, which is routinely linked to their ethnicity, last name, and physical appearance–a linguistic discrimination to which their White monolingual counterparts might not have been subject (Garcia and Kleifgen, 2018; Nieto and Bode, 2018).

Because of institutional and societal pressure to speak standard English, native and non-native Americans, including participants involved in this book, have taken accent reduction courses with speech therapists in order to improve and/or modify their English accent. While some people have tried to improve their accents to avoid experiencing accent discrimination, others have done so for professional advancement and social status (Blumenfeld, 2004; Sharp and Rowls, 2010). Indeed, famous media pundits and Hollywood figures have worked with speech therapists to help them acquire the desired or needed type of accent. A well-known speech therapist, Sam Chwat, worked directly with linguistic minorities and celebrity figures such as Isabella Rossellini, Willem Dafoe, Julia Roberts, and Danny Glover, who wanted to lose their accents to develop new ones for professional purposes.

Chwat also worked with news anchors from different regions in the United States to help them acquire what he called "unremarkable ways of speech". In an interview with Terry Gross, host of the NPR radio show Fresh Air, Chwat stated that many people contacted him because "they felt that their dialect distracted people from what they were saying" (Chwat, 1995). Chwat went on to say,

> Other reasons people come is because they find they're stigmatized for being members of a discriminated subgroup. They say, "I sound too black", "I sound too New York".... Or they feel that parts of their speech make them unintelligible or difficult to understand because most people are expecting standard American speech, which is an easier pattern most people understand.
>
> (Chwat, interviewed by Gross, 1995)

Accent discrimination is a serious sociolinguistic issue that is worth examining. Linguistically minoritized groups have been discriminated against in schools, and have been denied employment and promotion because of their noticeable non-standard accents (Baugh, 2018; Lippi-Green, 2012). Even those for whom English is their native tongue face accent discrimination, which is more often than not linked to their ethnicity, social class, and country of origin. This book sheds light on these timely issues.

Book Objective

Drawing from case studies conducted at different times over the course of five years, this book seeks to examine various ways in which minoritized linguistic groups have experienced accent discrimination in American schools and society at large. It provides insights into the insidious ways in which accent discrimination might have psychologically, academically, and professionally affected linguistically minoritized bilingual college students, professors, and other professionals. It goes on to highlight the degree to which their native language, ethnicity, and country of origin might have influenced the way they experienced accent discrimination.

A qualitative method was used to collect data for this book. The data consist of narratives written over a five-year span by bilingual and multilingual students and professors from various linguistic, ethnic, racial, and social-class backgrounds and countries of origin. Case studies are mostly about individuals for whom English was their second tongue; they spoke English with various accents deviating from the standard American English accent. A set of questions was designed and sent to participants asking them to share possible personal, academic, and professional challenges they might have faced because of their accent. In their narratives, participants referred to family members, friends, and classmates they witnessed being subjected to accent discrimination, in addition to their personal experiences with it. This book analyzes such experiences, including participants' linguistic resilience and resistance to succumbing to standard English accent supremacy.

Overview of the Book Chapters

The first three chapters that follow draw from several case studies to explore ways in which accent discrimination has affected linguistic minority groups, including bilingual college students and professionals, across social class, race, ethnicity, and country of origin. the last two chapters unpack the effects of accent and language hegemony on linguistic minorities living in both western and developing countries. The book as a whole demonstrates how accent hegemony has silenced other English accents, leading to discrimination against those speaking in non-dominant accents.

Summary

This book documents how accent discrimination occurs in schools and other institutions affecting linguistic minorities. It argues that accent discrimination affects linguistic minorities across language, race, ethnicity, social class, nationality, and gender. Those who speak English "with an accent" have often been denied opportunities, including employment, housing, and job promotion (Baugh, 2018; Lippi-Green, 2012). Very limited opportunities in institutions such as the mainstream media have been given to those who speak English with a noticeable non-standard accent. For example, television hosts and anchors in the United States have historically been those who speak with the so-called standard American or British accent. It is not [much] different in institutions such as universities and colleges, where one rarely finds individuals who speak English "with an accent" occupying key administrative positions, like provost or president. Denying people opportunities because of their accent–something they do not have control over–is a violation of their basic human right. This book aims to raise awareness about accent discrimination and its effects on linguistic minorities, including multilingual students and professionals.

References

Anzaldua, G. (1990). How to tame a wild tongue. In: R. Ferguson, M. Gever, T. Minh-Ha. & C. West (Eds.), *Out there: Marginalization and contemporary cultures* (pp. 24–44). Cambridge, MA: MIT Press.

Baugh, J. (2000). *Beyond Ebonics: Linguistic Pride and Racial Prejudice*. Oxford: Oxford University Press.

Baugh, J. (2018). *Linguistics in Pursuit of Justice*. Cambridge: Cambridge University Press.

Blumenfeld, R. (2004). *Accents: A Manual for Actors* (Revised and Expanded edition). New York: Limelight Editions.

Bourdieu, P. (1999). Language and Symbolic power. In: Adam Jaworski & Nikolas Coupland (Eds.), *The discourse reader* (pp. 502–514). London: Routledge.

Cabral, A. (1973). *Return to the source: Selected speeches by Amilcar Cabral*. New York: Monthly Review Press.

Canagarajah, AS. (1993). Critical ethnography of a Sri Lankan classroom: Ambiguities in student opposition to reproduction in ESOL. *TESOL Quarterly*, 27: 601–626.

Chomsky, N. (2013). *Topics in the Theory of Generative Grammar* (Vol. 56). Berlin, Germany: Walter de Gruyter.

Chomsky, N. (2014). *Aspects of the Theory of Syntax* (Vol. 11). Cambridge, MA: MIT Press.

Crawford, J. (2008). *Advocating for English Learners: Selected Essays*. Clevedon: Multilingual Matters.

Cummins, J. (2016). Reflections on Cummins (1980), "The Cross-Lingual Dimensions of Language Proficiency: Implications for Bilingual Education and the Optimal Age Issue". *TESOL Quarterly*, 50(4): 940–944.

DeGraff, M. (Ed.). (2001). *Language Creation and Language Change: Creolization, Diachrony, and Development.* Cambridge, MA: MIT Press.

DeGraff, M. (2003). Against Creole Exceptionalism. *Language*, 79(2): 391–410.

DeGraff, M. (2018). Error Correction and Social Transformation in Creole Studies and Among Creole Speakers: The Case of Haiti. *Language in Society*, 47(3): 354–360.

Dei, S. G. & Kempf. A. (2006). *Anti-colonialism and education.* Sense Publishers: Rotterdam/Taipei.

Fanon, F. (2008). *Black skin, white masks.* New York: Grove press.

Freire, P. (2020). *Pedagogy of the Oppressed.* London: Bloomsbury Publishing.

Gandhi, M. K. (1997). Hind Swaraj. In *Hind Swaraj and other writings.* Cambridge: Pearl.

Garcia, O., & Kleifgen, J. (2018). *Educating Emergent Bilinguals: Policies, Programs, and Practices for English Learners.* New York: Teachers College Press.

García, O., & Lin, A. M. (2017). Translanguaging in Bilingual Education. In *Bilingual and Multilingual Education* (pp. 117–130). New York: Routledge.

Gee, James Paul. (2014). "Decontextualized language: A problem, not a solution." *International Multilingual Research Journal*, 8(1): 9–23.

Gilyard, K. (2011). *True to the Language Game: African American Discourse, Cultural Politics, and Pedagogy.* New York: Routledge.

Gluszek, A., & Dovidio, J. F. (2010). The Way They Speak: Stigma of Non-Native Accents in Communication. *Personality and Social Psychology Review*, 14: 214–237.

James, C. L. R. (1989). *The Black Jacobins.* New York: Vintage.

Labov, W. (2011). *Principles of Linguistic Change, Cognitive and Cultural Factors* (Vol. 3). New York: John Wiley & Sons.

Lippi-Green, R. (2012). *English with an Accent: Language, Ideology and Discrimination in the United States* (2nd edition). New York: Routledge.

Macedo, D. (Ed.). (2019). *Decolonizing Foreign Language Education: The Misteaching of English and Other Colonial Languages.* New York: Routledge.

Macedo, D., Dendrinos, B., & Gounari, P. (2003). *The Hegemony of English.* Boulder, CO: Paradigm Publisher.

Marvasti, A. (2005). U.S. Academic Institutions and Perceived Effectiveness of Foreign-Born Faculty. *Journal of Economic Issues*, 39: 151–176.

Matsuda, M. J. (1991). Voices of America: Accent, Antidiscrimination Law, and a Jurisprudence for the Last Reconstruction. *Yale Law Journal*, 100: 1329–1407.

McLeod, J. (2001). *Beginning postcolonialism.* Manchester University Press.

Nieto, S. (2002). *Language, Culture, and Teaching: Critical Perspectives for a New Century.* New York: Lawrence Erlbaum Associates.

Nieto, S., & Bode, P. (2018). *Affirming Diversity: The Socio-Cultural Context of Multicultural Education.* Boston: Pearson Education, Inc.

Nyerere, J. (1968). *Ujamaa: Essays on socialism.* Dar es Salem: Oxford University Press.

Orelus, P. W., Malott, C. S., & Pacheco, R. (Eds.). (2014). *Colonized Schooling Exposed: Progressive Voices for Transformative Educational and Social Change*. New York: Routledge.

Orelus, P. W. (2020). Other People's English Accents Matter: Challenging Standard English Accent Hegemony. *Excellence in Education Journal*, 9(1): 120–148.

Pennycook, A. (2017). *The Cultural Politics of English as an International Language*. New York: Taylor & Francis.

Phillipson, R. (1992). *Linguistic Imperialism*. Oxford: Oxford University Press.

Phillipson, R. (2013). *Linguistic Imperialism Continued*. New York: Routledge.

Pratt, M. I. (1999). Arts of the contact zone. In: D. Bartholome (Ed.). *Ways of reading: An anthology for writers*. Boston: St. Matins (5th ed.).

Rodney, W. (2018). *How europe underdeveloped africa*. New York: Verso Books.

Sharp, E., & Rowls, H. J. (2010). *How to Do Accents*. London: Oberon Books.

Smith, L. T. (2019). *Decolonizing research: Indigenous storywork as methodology*. London: Bloomsbury Publishing.

Spring, J. (2019). *American education*. New York: Routledge.

Torres, M. (2004). To the Margins and Back: The High Cost of Being Latina in America. *Journal of Latinos and Education*, 3(2): 123–141.

Villegas, A. M. (1988). School failure and cultural mismatch: Another view. *The Urban Review*, 20(4): 253–263.

Wa Thiong'o, N. (1986). *Decolonising the mind: The politics of language in African literature*. London: James Currey.

Wane, N. N. (2006). Is Decolonization Possible? In: Sefa, G. J. & Kempf, A. *Anticolonialism and Education: The politics of resistance* (pp. 87–106). Rotterdam/Taipei: Sense Publishers.

2 All English Accents Matter

Around the world, English is spoken with a variety of accents. However, due to the legacy of linguistic imperialism, American and British English accents remain the most valued ones (Phillips, 1992). Specifically, because of social status accorded to so-called standard English accents, those whose accents are different are often ill-perceived and treated unjustly in society.

Indeed, linguistic minorities who speak with a different English accent routinely face "linguistic profiling" (Baugh, 2018). As for immigrants, they are often blamed for not trying hard enough to learn the standard American English accent regardless of their life circumstances (Lippi-Green, 2012; Neuliep and Speten-Hansen, 2013; Wolfram and Schilling, 2015). Speaking English with an identifiable non-dominant English accent often presents a problem for linguistically and culturally diverse groups in the United States, including bilingual students and professionals (Garcia and Kleifgen, 2018; Nieto and Bode, 2018). Nonetheless, these groups have faced such challenges with much resilience.

This chapter draws on several case studies and the work of postcolonial theorists and sociolinguists (Baugh, 2018; Thiong'o, 1986) to examine ways in which English speakers from diverse linguistic, ethnic, and cultural backgrounds and countries of origin have been subject to accent discrimination. While some participants directly experienced this systemic linguistic oppression, others witnessed family members, classmates, and family members being subjected to it. The intersection of participants' native language, ethnicity, and country of origin was explored, as the case studies aimed to highlight the role such intersection played in various forms and the degrees to which they experienced accent discrimination.

Language and Accent Identity

There is a tendency in mainstream society to focus on one form of identity and sideline others to the margins, even though research shows that all forms of identities intersect and impact our lives (Crenshow, 2016; Omoniyi, 2016). For instance, an individual might be privileged in one context and disenfranchised in another, depending on whether or not their identity, including linguistic identity, is valued and respected. This is to say that individuals whose linguistic identities reflect the reality of, and fit into, the mainstream standard English accent tend to receive better treatment than those whose accents are looked down upon (Baugh, 2018). Specifically, in the United States, linguistic minorities, including immigrants, African Americans, and Latinx people, whose English accents differ from the standard American accent, experience accent discrimination (Baugh, 2018; Rosa and Flores, 2017). Linguistic minorities have faced linguistic discrimination partly because linguistically prejudiced individuals often assume that the latter are intellectually inferior because of their accent. As a consequence, they often do not receive the respect they deserve, despite their academic and professional accomplishments (Omoniyi, 2016; Rosa and Flores, 2017).

It is worth noting that it is not merely the native language of linguistic minority groups that has subjected them to accent discrimination in the United States and beyond. Other factors, such as their ethnicity and race, play an equal role. For example, Rosa and Flores (2017) examined in their study the manner in which Latinx people were routinely mistaken for Mexican immigrants and were treated as second-language English learners even though they were born and raised in the United States. Specifically, Rosa and Flores (2017) noted that the way many Latinx people spoke was often linked to their ethnicity as well as their immigrant status.

Minoritized linguistic groups often feel pressured to speak in standard American English accent in schools as well as at work in order to fit in, as it is the accent most valued in these institutions (Lippi-Green, 2012). However, when they return home from work or school, they switch back to the accent or language familiar to their family members, friends, or neighbors–something those from dominant linguistic groups do not have to do in order to fit in (Rosa and Flores, 2017). While this study is not arguing against standard accent, it draws from participants' heartfelt narratives to challenge the hegemony of the standard American English accent, pointing out its effects on English speakers from diverse linguistic and cultural backgrounds and countries of origin.

Study Design

The data for the case studies examined in this chapter stem from a graduate seminar course on language and literacies that I taught at a state university located in Las Cruces, New Mexico. Twelve students, from diverse cultural, linguistic, and ethnic backgrounds and nationalities, attended the seminar. The idea of conducting the case study stemmed from engaging classroom discussions about accent and language hegemony. After the semester ended, I sent an email invitation along with a consent form to students who attended the seminar, asking if they would volunteer to take part in the study. Although all attendees were invited to participate in the case study, only eight agreed to do so. While some wrote about their personal experiences with standard accent hegemony, others talked about classmates, friends, and family members they witnessed experiencing this form of domination. They expressed their opinion about these issues, drawing from personal, academic, and professional experiences.

Participants' Backgrounds

Individuals taking part in the case studies spoke in diverse forms of accented English. Specifically, while some were native speakers of English, others were dominant English speakers whose first language was, for example, Spanish. They were from Ecuador, Colombia, Puerto Rico, India, Ghana, Jamaica, and New Orleans (U.S.). Whereas, some were k-12 teachers, others were school administrators pursuing doctoral degrees. Their ages ranged from 30s to 50s, and they were at different stages in their academic and professional careers.

Data Analysis

From the whole dataset, two linguistic minoritized groups were selected, based on their experiences with accent discrimination. Since participants' native and dominant languages were English and Spanish, I compared and contrasted speakers of these two languages. This comparative analysis was done to underscore ways in which diverse English speakers might have been subjected to varying degrees of accent discrimination. I used narrative analysis drawing from Johnson's (2014) work in sociolinguistics to interpret and analyze the data.

Narrative analysis helps understand the personal and social world of the participants. Indeed, such analysis helps capture participants' varied experiences with language and accent discrimination as well as their views on it. Through this lens, I began the data analysis process by focusing on identifying specific themes emerging from participants' narratives. Patterns, variances, resemblances, and differences in participants' accounts about accent discrimination were noted. Carefully identified themes were highlighted to illuminate plausible connections between the accent discrimination the participants experienced and their first language, ethnicity, and country of origin.

Through narrative analysis, the root causes of accent discrimination and the degree to which it affected study participants surfaced. However, for validity and transparency purposes, I emailed participants the interpretation and analysis of their narratives to give them an opportunity to revisit their stories. Some added to comments made about their lived experiences with accent discrimination, while others simply confirmed and approved what was sent to them. Their narratives were divided into two units addressing their experiences with accent discrimination. The two groups of participants were divided by their native languages and ethnicities. Participants' real names have been omitted to protect their identity.

Analysis of Case Studies

Unit One: Participants Whose First Language is English

In this unit analysis, narratives across the dataset were used to examine ways and the degree to which study's participants might have experienced accent discrimination because of their diverse English accents. While for some, English is their first language, for others, it is their second language. Their cases draw attention to the fact that merely being a dominant speaker of English, even as one's first language, does not necessarily guarantee protection from accent discrimination. Mary's experience is a case in point.

Mary's Case

At the time of the study, Mary (pseudonym) was a former high school English teacher in her 30s pursuing a doctoral degree. She immigrated to the United States from Jamaica when she was 11 years old, and she has been living there ever since. Mary experienced English accent hegemony in American schools when she first moved to the United States. When asked to talk about her experience as an immigrant whose dominant and first language is English, Mary began by retracing her journey from her native Jamaica to the United States, and talked about schooling experiences during which she endured accent discrimination:

> I was born and raised in Jamaica. It hadn't occurred to me when I left Jamaica for the US that my dialect would somehow come to define so much of my social and academic identities. Almost immediately as I arrived, my teacher wanted to place me in a bi-lingual class, never

mind that I spoke English. My accent was enough to distinguish me as a non-standard English speaker. (My teacher thought I was speaking French creole).

Mary's narrative unveils the extent to which schoolteachers, consciously or not, often impose the hegemony of standard American English accent on linguistically minoritized groups speaking in distinct English accents. Like many immigrants of color from formerly colonized English-speaking countries, Mary found herself being caught between two accented English worlds. In Jamaica, her middle-class English accent is accepted and treated as standard, whereas in the United States it is seen and treated as a problem that needs immediate remedy, rather than as a linguistic asset to cherish, maintain, and build on to effectively and efficiently teach her.

As soon as Mary's teachers realized that Mary had a distinct English accent, which, according to Mary, was not even recognized as English, she was placed in a bilingual program to learn English even though she already spoke it.

> The complexity of my language experience has made me realize that I sort of exist in an imperfect speech place. I can no longer master my first dialect, and yet I am still not able to master the standard variety I engage with daily. I am self-conscious often, especially because unlike my friends who do speak other languages, English is my first language.

Mary is not the only participant who experienced accent discrimination in American schools despite the fact that English is her first and dominant language. Other speakers of English, born and raised in former British colonies like India and Ghana, are also targeted because of their distinct English accents, as Aviva's case illuminates.

Aviva's Case

Aviva (pseudonym) is an immigrant from India. She earned her first master's degree in Bengali, one of the languages spoken in her native land. While living in India, she taught literature at the Visva-Bharati University founded by the Nobel laureate poet and educator Rabindranath Tagore. After immigrating to North America–Canada and then the United States– some 30 years ago, she obtained her second master's degree in English at a state university. Aviva was Assistant Professor of Rhetoric and Composition at a community college located in the southwestern United States while pursuing a doctoral degree in language, literacy, and culture at a U.S. university. Aviva talked about her experience with accent discrimination:

> A lady is there sitting by me. She and I, too, begin chit-chatting about this and that. Where are you from? Kolkata, India. Oh, how I love talking about my country and my hustling and bustling city! What brings you here? Well, my husband's work. The questioning continues: What do you do? I tell her I teach English at the community college here in town. She pauses, stares at me, and breaks into a laugh. I don't hear the hum anymore.

Aviva's typical South Asian English accent instantly made her become a marker, a foreigner, or simply an outsider. Aviva was approached by this woman, who at first showed curiosity to know her, and then went on to ridicule her distinctive English accent. Aviva, who grew up speaking English in her native land and who has lived in two English-speaking countries, Canada and the United States, continued to face insensitive linguistic comments from both random individuals and her students because of her English accent. Aviva continued:

> Suddenly, the world around me falls silent while her laugh in my head keeps on ringing and ringing. Sometimes students, those who do not do well in my composition course, leave comments in course evaluation stating that they do not understand the subject content of what I teach because of my accent. These comments, however, are few and far between.

It does not seem to matter that Aviva is an English college professor who is pursuing a doctoral degree; she is still prone to insensitive linguistic comments about her English accent. Like Mary, Aviva is caught between two accented English worlds without her choosing, and she is not alone. other English-speaking immigrants, like Jack, from a formerly British colony, Ghana, have faced similar linguistic challenges.

Jack's Case

Jack (pseudonym), a 23-year-old college student, is from West Africa. Jack was born in Ghana, and he grew up in a middle-class family. Although Twi is one of the dialects spoken in his tribal group, Jack grew up speaking English, which has been his dominant language, particularly since he moved to the United States. Jack stated that his English accent was considered and treated as foreign in comparison to standard American English accent, particularly when he first moved the United States.

Like other immigrants, Jack moved to the United States to go to college pursuing his dream. At the time of the study, he was in his second year in college. Jack explained how he felt when he was discriminated against in class because of his distinctive English accent:

> When I first started college–I had been at the United States only for a couple of months–my accent was very different. Every time I tried to ask questions in class, I could see some of the students giggling. This continued for a while, which made me feel embarrassed and never wanted to utter a word again in class.

Jack was tongue-tied in class. He feared his classmates would make fun of his English accent. Jack's accent was very different when he first started school in the United States, and his peers laughed at it each time he asked questions in class. Facing this form of discrimination must have been frustrating for Jack as an immigrant who grew up speaking English as one of his dominant languages. However, his instructor intervened and tried to stop his peers from bullying him. Jack says, "But the class instructor stepped in and warned those students. I was always overwhelmed with fear when homework, particularly oral presentation, was due, because I didn't know how my classmates would react to my English accent".

Like Mary's and Aviva's experiences, Jack's accent discrimination experience shows that growing up speaking English as one's first or dominant dialect does not automatically guarantee historically disenfranchised individuals' or groups' protection from accent discrimination. Like Jack and Aviva, Jen, an African American university professor, was subjected to accent discrimination at a store despite the fact that English is her first and only language.

Jen's Case

Jen (a pseudonym) was born and raised in New Orleans. She is African American. She earned all three of her degrees in Louisiana. She is currently a tenured professor at a university located in the southwestern United States. At the time of the accent incident, she was working on her doctorate in education administration and was considered middle-class. This was a first-time event. Until then, most people commented on how much she did not sound like she was from New Orleans, so to now be told that she could not be understood because of her accent was news to her.

> All my life, I have hated my voice. I am from New Orleans, and I am reminded often that I do not sound like I am from New Orleans. I guess

that could be a compliment, but I am never sure. When I lived in the Northeast, the students told me that they could not tell that I was from the South. However, my husband's Southern accent is more pronounced than mine, and he received negative feedback regularly. My challenge came once when I wore a decorative head wrap to a car dealership. One of my students had visited Greece and bought me a wrap. I was launching a complaint in the car dealership, and I thought I was very clear about my complaint. I thought I had been charged for a diagnostic that was attributed to a recalled part. I thought I should not have to pay the diagnostic fee, so I requested a refund. The White woman became very angry and called over a Hispanic guy to "deal with me" because I wasn't speaking English.

The manager appeared to have assumed that Jen was an immigrant possibly because of her speech pattern, that is, her African American Vernacular English (AAVE) accent combined with the African attire she was wearing. African Americans, particularly those from the South, speak in African American Vernacular English accent. However, Jen stated that people, including students, could not figure out whether she was from the South based on her accent. Nonetheless, she was discriminated against. Jen added:

> I was disturbed by that because the only thing I think she did was look at the ethnic head wrap and made assumptions about my ethnicity. I explained to the gentleman that I was not sure which language she thought I was speaking, but I assured him that English was my primary language.

American African vernacular (AAVE) is a language that plays a fundamental role in cultural and historical aspects of African Americans' lives. Yet, AAVE has hitherto been constructed as a dialect inferior to Standard American English–a view challenged by linguists like Gilyard (2011), who states:

> Linguistics teaches us that African American Vernacular English (AAVE) is a legitimate language variety in its own right. It is not a broken version of any other verbal system and has the same standing among linguists as any other variety of language, be it an English version or otherwise. Like spoken languages worldwide, AAVE is fully conceptual; is composed of between ten to seventy meaningful sounds; has rules of syntax; and contains statements, commands, questions, and exclamations.
>
> (p. 53)

That AAVE accent is inferior to the standard American English accent is a faulty claim in that, up until now, no scientific research has proven that a particular language or accent is superior to or better than another (Baugh, 2018; Green, 2002; Labov, 2011; Skutnabb-Kangas and Philipson, 2016; Wolfram and Schilling, 2015). Participants' cases show that speaking English, even as one's first or dominant language, does not necessarily exempt one from accent discrimination, and that being discriminated against because of one's English accent also depends on underlying factors, such as one's race, ethnicity, and country of origin, as the following narratives illustrate.

Unit 2: Narratives of Participants Whose First Language is Spanish

This unit contains the stories of participants whose first language is Spanish but grew up speaking English as their second and dominant language before moving to the United States. Like participants for whom English is their first language, they were discriminated against because of their accent, as shown in the following narratives.

Juan's Case

Juan (a pseudonym) was born and raised in Puerto Rico. He grew up speaking English as his second language. After finishing high school in Puerto Rico, Juan moved to the mainland, the United States, to pursue graduate studies. Juan is currently teaching history at a university located in New York; he has been a professor for over a decade. He has been subject to accent discrimination as both a graduate student and a professor. Juan has experienced this form of discrimination in both his first language, Spanish, and his second language, English. Juan maintained, "At the university, the discrimination came from a professor who not only wrote in my first evaluation that my accent in English made me difficult to understand but who also rejected my Spanish because she was used to 'Colombian and Mexican Spanish which were superior to Caribbean Spanish.'" Juan elaborated:

> Mind you that she was not fluent in Spanish, not really. And that Spanish was my only language for 22 years, and my BA-granting institution was Spanish-language-based. Finally, though the hundreds of students I had in Rutgers and UMass never complained about my accent, one semester at Marist College (New York), in a particularly difficult section, some five students, aware that they were failing the class, banded together and stated in their class evaluations that to improve the class they should "hire an American who spoke English to teach it" and several variations of that comment. I suspect that had something to do with not having my contract renewed next year.

Juan was reminded that his Spanish was not standard enough to be understood and to earn the respect of his professor. The irony is that Spanish is neither the first nor dominant language of this professor, but she deems Juan's Caribbean Spanish accent to be inferior to the Colombian and Mexican Spanish accents to which she is mostly accustomed.

Juan not only faced accent discrimination from his professor because of his Spanish Caribbean accent; he also received unfavorable student course evaluations, apparently because of students' prejudice against his English accent. Juan claimed that his teaching contract was terminated because students complained about his accent. Juan's experience shows that defenders of the hegemony of standard accents can be linguistically insensitive to those who speak in different accents. In this professor's view, Juan's Spanish accent, originating from Puerto Rico, sounds foreign and incomprehensible, even though such accent reflects Juan's linguistic and social identities. Juan's accent is part of a variety of Spanish accents–some of which are socially constructed as standard, while others are seen and treated as non-standard. Juan was frustrated and disappointed; he felt discriminated against by a university language professor, whom one would expect to be linguistically sensitive and accepting.

Juan's experience is different from that of Pablo, who is from Spain. Even though they are both Spanish speakers and English second-language learners, they experienced accent discrimination differently. Their ethnicity and race play a role in their linguistic experiences in the United States.

Pablo's Case

Pablo (pseudonym) was born and raised in Spain. He is married and has three children who are bilingual. Pablo is mixed; his mother is Spanish, while his father is an immigrant from Ecuador. Pablo, a former EFL (English as a foreign language) teacher, was an assistant professor at a west-coast university at the time of this study. He immigrated to the United States to work as a Spanish teacher.

He then pursued graduate studies after years of teaching in both his native land and the United States. Upon finishing his doctoral studies, he pursued and secured a university faculty position. Pablo stated that in many of his encounters in the United States and Europe, people made positive comments about his Spanish accent, while looking down on that of his wife, who is from Ecuador.

> People seem to celebrate more some countries over others, same as they do with races. They probably celebrate some countries over others influenced by country variables. When some people have asked me

where I'm from and when I say Spain, some of them seem to kind of celebrate. However, when they ask my wife, who is from Ecuador, I notice they don't celebrate anything.

Pablo's narrative further illustrates unequal power relations between standard Spaniard Spanish accent and Latin American Spanish accents. People who are from Spain and speak in standard Spanish accents tend to be seen through positive linguistic lenses, whereas those from former colonized Spanish territories are often perceived and treated poorly. This linguistic disparity is connected to the persistent effects of the Spanish colonial legacy on Latin America, as linguistically diverse individuals from Latin America and the Caribbean are often ridiculed because of their marked accents. Pablo added:

> Although some people probably celebrate because they know more about Spain than about Ecuador, it seems that same as race (people in Spain are lighter than in Ecuador, a country that is more associated to Indigenous peoples), ethnicity (the culture in Spain is better considered than the culture in Ecuador), class (a European country versus a third-world country), and language (some people tell me about the Castilian Spanish and insist that the Spanish from Spain is the correct and formal Spanish and that Spanish in Latin America is wrong, informal, and non-educated).

Because of the European colonial legacy, Spanish accents from Latin America and the Caribbean are treated as low-class. This complicates the accent matter. The colonial legacy lingers on and, consequently, places formerly colonized people from Latin America in disadvantageous linguistic position, as Linda's case further illustrates.

Linda's Case

Linda (pseudonym) was a doctoral candidate at a flagship university located in the midwestern United States at the time of the study. She was born and raised in a city near the Atlantic Coast of Colombia, so Spanish is her first language. She got her undergraduate education in Colombia and started learning French, which became her second language. By the end of her graduate studies, she decided to focus on learning English only, so her French was not used much, and it was quickly forgotten.

She lived and taught English as a foreign language in Europe, Asia, and Central and South America before coming to the U.S. to pursue graduate studies. She considers herself multilingual, as she has studied at least five languages throughout her life. Linda was pursuing a master's degree at a university located in the southwestern United States at the time of the study. Linda stated that one of the most painful acts of discrimination she endured over the years was connected to her distinctive accent.

> When I think about any experiences with accent discrimination throughout my personal and professional journey, many incidents come to mind. As the coordinator of a children's program, I was in charge of overseeing groups of young volunteers from different states in the U.S. These undergraduate students spent their summer helping with our summer ESL camps. I specifically remember one of the volunteers telling me how "thick" my accent was in English and how difficult it was for him to understand me.

Linda was looked down on not only because of her accent but also because of her ethnicity and nationality—a brown-skinned woman from Latin America with a "foreign, Spanish-sounding English accent". The White male American student that Linda referred to in her narrative was convinced that Linda was not and could not be qualified to be the coordinator of that program because of her non-standard English accent. Linda, on the other hand, found his behavior and attitude toward her distinct accent to be discriminatory and biased. Linda went on to say:

> From that incident, I particularly remember the emphatic way in which this male White American student made me feel that, no matter how qualified and professionally capable I was as an ESL teacher, my English language skills were not good enough because I didn't have a native accent.

White native-born Americans might not face institutional challenges teaching English as a second or foreign language, the competence of qualified non-native-speaker teachers of English is often questioned. Linda was reminded that her accent did not sound like the typical American English accent; therefore, she could not possibly be qualified to be the coordinator of a program that required strong communication English skills. Regardless of her competence as a coordinator and teacher, Linda's authority was interrogated and doubted because she spoke in a distinct English accent similar to that of many linguistic minorities in the Unites States.

Linda felt that she was discriminated against because she is a brown Latina whose English accent is constructed as colloquial. However, the final participant's narrative in this unit challenges Linda's assumption about the unearned linguistic privileges associated with merely growing speaking English as one's first and dominant language.

Claudia's Case

Claudia (pseudonym) is a Chicana who was born in El Paso, Texas. She is a third-generation U.S.-born citizen. She is bilingual and bicultural and attended public elementary, middle, and high schools in El Paso. She grew up speaking both the English and Spanish languages because her mother spoke Spanish and only understood English (She was an immigrant from Mexico), and her father spoke English but understood Spanish. She and her brother benefitted greatly from their mother, with whom they spoke Spanish, while speaking only English with their father. Claudia has a B.A. in political science, an M.A. in higher education, and a Ph.D. in educational leadership with a focus on higher education. She is currently a high-school college counselor and academic advisor. What follows is Claudia's experience with accent discrimination.

> I have been told, time and again, that it's surprising I speak my English without a "Mexican" accent and that I pronounce words "so well" as if pronouncing them with a different accent would interrupt their wellness. In true form to my Chicana experience, living in the liminal space of neither here nor there, I have similarly been told by Spanish speakers that it is unfathomable that I speak Spanish so properly and without sounding like a "gringa".

Claudia's experience with accent discrimination underscores that linguistic privileges are also linked to one's ethnicity, race, and country of origin. Although Claudia is a third-generation U.S.-born citizen, she is still perceived and treated as a Mexican immigrant, a second-language English learner. Claudia received compliments from random individuals about both her English and Spanish accents, depending on the context and the circumstances. She was told that her English accent was very good, as if she was not expected to speak proper English. In other contexts, Spanish speakers were impressed with her oral Spanish skills, as though she was not expected to speak like them. Claudia's narrative suggests that she was mistaken for a Latina immigrant, a second-language learner who speaks good English.

Perhaps people expect that someone who is Chicana/Mexican American/ Latinx should sound like they have an accent from a specific geographic region, usually Mexico or elsewhere in Latin America. Simultaneously, those who do not expect Claudia to speak "good Spanish" presume that as an American, she should have an Anglicized accent and a limited vocabulary in Spanish. Claudia added:

> In people's assessment of my use of either language, I am positioned as different/other/anomaly. Otherwise, why point it out? Is it my sound or their hearing that is actually to be pointed out? The act of "correcting" is an act of pointing a finger, cornering, marginalizing, and putting someone in her place. It is an interruption to the storytelling, an attempt to manipulate the narration, and a hyper act of situating someone away from the center, even of her own story.

In both situations, the problem is other people's specific and erroneous presumptions about Claudia and what it means to be of her ethnicity, instead of her inability to speak a language.

General Discussion

Accent discrimination has affected not only second-language English learners but also minority speakers for whom English is their first language. For example, although English is Claudia's first and dominant language, she was perceived and treated as a second-class citizen, a second-language English learner. As for Jen, she was treated as if she could not make herself understood to the manager at the retail store in English, the only language she knows. The manager felt that she had to call another minority, a Spanish guy, to deal with Jen, supposedly because she could not understand her accent. What this manager seemingly failed to realize is that, like Jen, everybody has an accent, including her. Instead of discriminating against Jen, this manager could have inquired about her accent. This inquiry could have generated conversations about language and accent diversity, including regional accents, while at the same time creating space for human closeness and bonding between her, the manager, and Jen, the customer. Unfortunately, this manager, who apparently believed in racial and linguistic stereotypes, ill-treated Jen linguistically, an educated African American woman.

Similarly, Mary, who grew up as a middle-class English speaker with a Jamaican English accent, was placed in a bilingual classroom to learn proper English upon the recommendation of one of her schoolteachers. It is unfair for English-speaking participants who grew up speaking English as their first language to face accent discrimination in the English language. In the case of Jen in particular, the manager assumed that, as a doctoral student, she was unable to make herself clear in English—a language she grew up speaking in Jamaica. Like African American

Vernacular English accent in the United States, Spanish accents from Latin America and the Caribbean, like those of Pablo's wife and Juan, are hierarchically assessed to be inferior to the Spaniard accent. This is linked to the colonial legacy that has historically influenced hierarchical power relations between dominant languages and marginalized ones.

Conclusion and Policy Implications

Participants' narratives underscore how and the degree to which accent discrimination has affected minorities across native languages, ethnicities/races, nationalities, and countries of origin. Their narratives suggest much work needs to be done for accent diversity and inclusion to become a reality for linguistically and culturally disenfranchised groups whose distinct English accents do not fit the standard American accent label. Because of their distinct English accents, these groups frequently face accent discrimination, whereas those whose accents fit such standard are often praised and placed on a higher linguistic pedestal

As the United States becomes increasingly linguistically and culturally diverse, there is a need for institutionalized anti-colonial language policies that protect the linguistic rights of linguistic minority groups. Such policies should enable all people to speak in accents that deviate from the so-called standard American English accent without being subjected to accent discrimination. In institutions like schools and the workplace, professional workshops and seminars on accent and language diversity need to be offered, in which attendees could acquire knowledge and develop understanding and sensitivity about various speech patterns that have shaped different English speakers from diverse linguistic communities across the United States and beyond.

Such workshops or seminars would help attendees acquire knowledge about, and develop understanding of, diverse accents and the cultural and linguistic speech patterns among various linguistic minorities. Teachers need to embrace in their classrooms various accents spoken by students of diverse linguistic backgrounds. More specifically, teachers must interact with, and show genuine curiosity about, students speaking with different accents. This will serve as a model for other students, by making them less likely to laugh at their classmates speaking with an accent different from the norm, but rather trying to engage them with genuine, reflective, and friendly curiosity in an inquisitive and respectful manner.

Teachers also need to make a genuine effort to incorporate in their lesson plans language-based activities focused on accent diversity. Doing so would help foster a classroom environment conducive to linguistic awareness about diverse English accents spoken around the world. Likewise, teachers need to engage monolingual English speaker students in such activities, as they might not have had much exposure to diverse accents and dialects growing up. Along the same lines, members of dominant linguistic groups need to be proactive seeking opportunities to interact with linguistic minorities so that they can develop awareness about different English accents. Finally, the social construction and imposition of an American standard English accent must be challenged, for it constitutes an obstacle to accent diversity and inclusion. There are many benefits in accepting and embracing accent diversity and inclusion, and there are teachers who respect, embrace, and accept different languages and accents in their classrooms (Nieto and Bode, 2018). However, more work needs to be done to ensure the acceptance of, and respect for, diverse English accents.

References

Baratta, A. (2017). Accent and Linguistic Prejudice within British Teacher Training. *Journal of Language, Identity and Education*, 1–8.

Baugh, J. (2003). Linguistic Profiling. *Black Linguistics: Language, Society, and Politics in Africa and the Americas*, 1(1): 155–168.

Baugh, J. (2018). *Linguistics in Pursuit of Justice*. Oxford, England: Cambridge University Press.

Cervantes-Soon, C. (2012). Testimonios of Life and Learning in the Borderlands: Subaltern Juarez Girls Speak. *Equity & Excellence in Education*, 45(3): 373–391.

De Costa, P. I. (2010). Language Ideologies and Standard English Language Policy in Singapore: Responses of a 'Designer Immigrant' Student. *Language Policy*, 9(3): 217–239.

Delgado Bernal, D. et al. (2012). Chicana/Latina Testimonios: Mapping the Methodological, Pedagogical, and Political. *Equity & Excellence in Education*, 45(3): 363–372.

Eisenchlas, S. A., & Tsurutani, C. (2011). You Sound Attractive! Perceptions of Accented English in a Multilingual Environment. *Australian Review of Applied Linguistics*, 34(2): 216–236.

Green, L. J. (2002). *African American English: A Linguistic Introduction*. New York: Cambridge University Press.

Johnson, D. E. (2014). *Quantitative Methods in Sociolinguistics*. Summer School 5 University College Dublin.

Labov, W. (2011). *Principles of Linguistic Change, Cognitive and Cultural Factors* (Vol. 3). New York: John Wiley & Sons.

Lippi-Green, R. (2012). *English with an Accent: Language, Ideology and Discrimination in the United States* (2nd edition). New York: Routledge.

Neuliep, J. W., & Speten-Hansen, K. M. (2013). The Influence of Ethnocentrism on Social Perceptions of Nonnative Accents. *Language & Communication*, 33(3): 167–176.

Nieto, S., & Bode, P. (2018). *Affirming Diversity: The Sociopolitical Context of Multicultural Education* (7th edition). New York: Pearson.

Omoniyi, T. (2016). Language, Race, and Identity. In: P. Siân (Ed.), *The Routledge Handbook of Language and Identity*. New York: Routledge.

Phillips, R. (1992). *Linguistic Imperialism*. Oxford: Oxford University Press.

Rosa, J., & Flores, N. (2017). Unsettling Race and Language. Toward a Raciolinguistic Perspective. *Language in Society*, 46(5): 621–647.

Skutnabb-Kangas, T., & Philipson, R. (Eds.). (2016). *Language Rights*. New York: Routledge.

Wolfram, W., & Schilling, N. (2015). *American English: Dialects and Variation* (Vol. 25). New York: John Wiley & Sons.

3 Affirming Accent Variation

Accent discrimination rarely comes to the forefront of political and educational debates centered around social-justice issues, even though it is a systemic oppression that affects our day-to-day lives. One's accent is often influenced by one's linguistic, socio-economic, ethnic, and regional identities; these factors, in turn, psychologically and socio-cognitively influence one's pitch (high or low), inflection, rhythm and, above all, speech pattern (Baugh, 2018; Labov, 2011; Levy and Crowley, 2012). When individuals or groups enunciate words in ways deviating from the socially constructed standard accent, they are often labeled as speaking with an accent, often resulting in discrimination against them (Lippi-Green, 1994, 2012; Livingston et al., 2016; Nelson et al., 2016).

Linguistic discrimination infringes on the inalienable right of minority groups to speak their mother tongue in accents deviating from the alleged standard English accent. Baugh (2018) examines the salient effects of various kinds of accent discrimination, including linguistic profiling, on minority groups, particularly African Americans, in American schools and society. Bilingual and multicultural scholars and researchers have also examined various effects of accent discrimination on linguistic minorities, including emerging bilingual students (i.e., Nieto and Bode, 2018). This book draws from the sociolinguistic work of these scholars and participants' *testimonios* to underscore various ways in which linguistic minorities, including bilingual students and professors across ethnicity and language, have experienced systemic accent discrimination.

According to Cervantes et al. (2019), "*Testimonios* allow individuals to name their realities and to share specific experiences of oppression or trauma that they have endured" (p. 2). Scholars from different backgrounds and with different foci in the academy have used *testimonios* to challenge the master narrative, asserting themselves in the world in their own voice and words. Indeed, historically oppressed groups in both developing and

DOI: 10.4324/9781315858135-3

under-developing countries have used *testimonios* as a form of resistance to systemic oppression. *Testimonios* emerge from and reflect people's daily living and breathing realities. According to Delgado Bernal and colleagues (2012), *testimonios* have been "giving voice to silences, representing the other, reclaiming authority to narrate, and disentangling questions surrounding legitimate truth" (p. 365.)

Testimonios of linguistic minorities from diverse ethnic and cultural backgrounds are used to underscore various ways in which they have been subjected to systemic forms of accent discrimination, or accentism for short. Accentism is defined here as a dominant ideology that favors accents constructed as standard over others labeled as lower or inferior class, leading to accent discrimination against minoritized linguistic groups. In other words, minoritized linguistic groups speaking with an English accent deviating from the standard American English accent are routinely subjected to accentism. By contrast, those who speak in standard accent are often assumed to be smart or smarter, educated, and given the benefit of the doubt about their intelligence (Baugh, 2018; Lippi-Green, 2012; Matsuda, 1991).

Accentism

Accentism is interwoven with underlying factors, such as ethnicity, race, and social class. For instance, although African Americans are native speakers of English, they have been discriminated against for speaking Ebonics (Baugh, 2018; Labov, 2011; Lippi-Green, 2012). Ebonics is rooted in the history of African Americans, including the Atlantic slave trade. Enslaved Africans came from different tribes, spoke various dialects, and intermingled with other enslaved Africans during this trade. Through such interaction, the captured Africans were exposed to new dialects, influencing their native languages along with their accents. This colonial legacy has influenced African American Vernacular English as well as the way African Americans have been ill-perceived and treated in comparison to those who speak so-called standard American English.

The inferiority construction of African American Vernacular English must be challenged in virtue of the fact that no scientific research has proven that certain accents or languages are superior to others (Baugh, 2010, 2018; Chomsky, 2013, 2014; Labov, 2011). Yet, for accentists–that is, those who discriminate against others based on their distinct accents–African Americans speaking Ebonics do not speak Standard English. As this book highlights, standard accent is a social construct. This construct has historically favored linguistically privileged groups over disenfranchised linguistic minorities speaking English with an accent (Lippi-Green, 2012).

42 *Affirming Accent Variation*

As highlighted in the previous chapter, acquiring a native-like accent in a dominant language does not necessarily guarantee that an individual or group, particularly those from marginalized linguistic, racial, and socioeconomic backgrounds, will be exempt from accent discrimination, for underlying factors, such as linguistic and ethnic heritage, nationality, and social class are intrinsically linked to accentism. This book demonstrates that the imposition of American standard English accent on disfranchised linguistic minority groups has affected them in ways that might have gone unrecognized.

Participants

A diverse bilingual and multilingual group, including international bilingual college students and professors and other professionals, participated in this book as subject participants. While some were U.S. natives, others were from other parts of the world, including Germany, Senegal, Colombia, Mexico, Eretria, and the Philippines. For some, English was their native tongue, while for others English was their second and dominant language–they were native speakers of Spanish, German, and French, among other languages. Furthermore, while some were k-12 school administrators and teachers pursuing doctoral degrees, others were university professors. Finally, their ages ranged from 20s to 60s at the time of the study, and they were at different stages in their academic and professional lives.

Data Collection

This chapter draws on *testimonios* collected from students and colleagues in different contexts and at different times across the United States. Some were garnered from classrooms of colleagues who agreed to help recruit students to take part in the study, while others stemmed from a workshop on accent discrimination and accent diversity designed for bilingual teachers, administrators, and parents that I was invited to conduct at a middle school in Las Cruces, New Mexico. A focus group of about 15 bilingual teachers, college students, university professors, and administrators participated in this workshop.

The workshop was attended primarily by linguistic-minority teachers, professors, and administrators working with bilingual students and English-language learners. While some personally experienced accent discrimination, others witnessed family members, friends, and neighbors being subjected to it. I designed the workshop in a way that created space for participants to talk about their experiences. After the workshop ended, I followed up with individuals who agreed to participate in the study.

While some participants chose to write about their personal experiences with accent discrimination, others talked about family members, classmates, and peers they witnessed being targeted and discriminated against because of their English accent. Some participants wrote their accounts during the workshop, while others wrote theirs much later. Data for this study consisted of participants' *testimonios* about experiences with accent discrimination as well as their ?views? on the subject.

Data Analysis

Participants were asked to share their *testimonios* about any form of accent discrimination they personally experienced or witnessed someone else (i.e., family members, co-workers, close friends, neighbors, classmates, or strangers) experiencing. Participants were also asked to talk about their positions on standard accent. The collected narratives were sorted by themes and analyzed accordingly.

Participants' various views on accents and personal experiences with accent discrimination across social class, ethnic, and racial backgrounds and nationality were also analyzed. A preliminary analysis of the whole data set was performed to determine which parts were relevant to the study.

Similarities, differences, restatements, and contradictions in participants' accounts were noted and analyzed. Some of the issues participants addressed were not directly connected to the focus of this case study; they at times talked about unrelated, yet important, issues that provided a broader scope of understanding of the issues at hand. I sorted participants' narratives by themes, from which units of data were carefully crafted and analyzed. In each unit, relevant information about study participants' background is provided.

Units of Data Analysis

Units of data analysis were formed based on both similarities and differences in themes emerging from participants' *testimonios*, as their experiences with accent discrimination varied. The first unit comprises *testimonios* in which study participants talked about their own experiences with and views of accent discrimination, The second unit contains *testimonios* of participants who indirectly experienced accent discrimination; they, for example, witnessed family members and peers being subjected to accent discrimination in schools and public places.

44   *Affirming Accent Variation*

In both units, attention is drawn to various ways in which people's biases and prejudices against linguistic minority groups, including bilingual college students and professors, might have affected the latter. Both units highlight various forms/types of accent discrimination against linguistic minorities, including immigrant French bilingual students from African countries,. Participants' *testimonios* bring to the forefront the roles ethnicity, nationality, and native language play in linguistic minorities' varying experiences of accent discrimination.

Unit One

Linguistic Minorities Experiencing Accent Discrimination: An Examination of the Causes and Effects

Vob's Case

Vob (pseudonym) was born in Germany and immigrated to the United States with his parents when he was 11 years old. He was in his early 20s and pursuing a master's degree at an east-coast university at the time of the study. Vob often received unpleasant treatment, including being subjected to interrogation, because of his perceived foreign English accent. Unlike his monolingual White American friends, he encounters accent discrimination while traveling. Vob states,

> I remember various instances wherein I felt that I was being profiled based on my accent alone. A simple, "Hi, how is it going", uttered by me was usually met with an agent's assertive "country of citizenship" or "where are you from" type of request. While I am happy to comply with their requests and understand that a lot of what they do simply has to do with following procedure, which usually results in my visa/passports being inspected and questions being asked, I feel that there must be a better way to communicate with people in my situation.

Vob finds remarks made and questions asked about his English accent to be linguistically biased and discriminatory. While his native-born White American friends and classmates face no accent challenges going through the checkpoint, Vob faces institutional linguistic hurdles going through the same process because of his accent. Vob adds,

> It is hard to explain how these exchanges go to my American friends because when we travel through the checkpoint together (or when they

Affirming Accent Variation 45

go through it alone), the whole process usually seems to be quite pleasant, speedy, and inconsequential. I think it is the mere idea of being recognized as someone who is different solely by the sound of my voice, and consequently being communicated with differently that makes me feel quite unwelcome and isolated in those moments.

Ethnically, Germans are not among the dominant minority groups in recent U.S. history. However, as a second-language English learner, he has been subjected to unpleasant linguistic discriminatory practices similar to those minorities and immigrants of color have faced in the United States. It seems as if all linguistic minorities have been subject to accent discrimination differently depending on their ethnicity, nationality, and country of origin, as well as the sociolinguistic context they find themselves in. Leanne's experience with accent discrimination is a case in point.

Leanne's Case

Leanne (pseudonym) was pursuing a doctorate degree at a state university located in the midwestern United States at the time of the study. She was in her 30s and born and raised in Colombia. In addition to her native Spanish, and English, which has become her second language, she studied French and other languages. Leanne considers herself bilingual but has studied at least five other languages. She has taught English as a foreign language overseas in different European and Asian countries. Because of her nonstandard English accent, Leanne has had several unpleasant accent discrimination experiences—one of which occurred with her boyfriend, who is a native speaker of standard English. Leanne narrates some of her experiences in the following terms:

> A person from Australia invited me to have dinner at her place. In this occasion, I went there with my boyfriend, who is American. The next time this person from Australia met my boyfriend, she asked him if we had communication issues in our relationship. She told him, "It must be very difficult for you to be in a relationship with someone who is not a native English speaker. Her accent is very strong". She was laughing about it. As you can imagine when my boyfriend told me, I did not find it funny at all. On the contrary, situations like that affected my personal and professional confidence.

Leanne felt offended by her boyfriend's friend's comment, which she did not find funny. The comment seems to have psychologically impacted her, particularly her confidence. Regardless of her sociolinguistic and cognitive abilities–as a Spanish native speaker, she has taught English as a foreign language overseas in different European and Asian countries–Leanne's accent was made fun of. Leanne's non-standard accent does not seem to be appreciated in mainstream monolingual American society. Leanne experienced other forms of accent discrimination connected to the first one. She goes on to add,

> As a native English speaker, my boyfriend had mentioned numerous times to me that in order to be taken seriously as a professional in this country, I had to do something about my accent. He reminded me about the incident with the Australian lady and recommended me to sign up for accent reduction therapy. So, for two years I went to the speech and hearing clinic to work on accent reduction. I'm not sure if the therapy helped to "reduce" my accent, but what I can say for sure is that I was always very aware of it, and I did not like to speak in front of groups of people because I was always very self-conscious about my accent.

Leanne was told that her accent did not sound like the typical American English accent that her boyfriend's friend expected to hear. As a result, she was pressured to take accent reduction courses by her boyfriend, who claimed that doing so would help her improve her English communication skills, which, in turn, would make people take her more seriously. This claim is questionable, however, linguistic minorities like African Americans, Latinx people, and Asians born and/or raised in the United States have been discriminated against because of their accents (Baugh, 2018; Lippi-Green, 2012). Abdel's narrative similarly suggests that factors such as ethnicity, race, and nationality are connected to accent discrimination.

Abdel's Case

Abdel (a pseudonym) was born and raised in Eritrea and moved to the United States in 1969 as a student on a government scholarship to pursue higher education and other opportunities. Specifically, he came here to complete a master's degree, which he started back home, in his field of study. Abdel spoke English before immigrating here, in addition to two other languages. In fact, he completed his undergraduate studies in English, as this was the language of instruction at the university in Ethiopia (Eritrea was part of Ethiopia at that time). He was a university professor in the U.S. at the time of the study. Because he spoke perfect English before moving to the United States, Abdel was shocked when people could not understand him.

He attributed this to what he called "his heavy Ethiopian/Eritrean accent". Abdel states,

> It was very frustrating when I had to repeat myself several times to be understood. I was an excellent student and my accent did not cause me much of a problem, although I was feeling the pain when I see my professors having a hard time understand me. But I have never experienced being discriminated against because of my accent. However, I suspect that I have missed some promotion opportunities due to my accent.

Abdel seems ambivalent in his statements about accent discrimination. On one hand, he claims that he was surprised that his peers and professors did not understand him because of his accent. On the other, he states, "I have never experienced being discriminated against because of my accent". He then goes on to say, "I suspect that I have missed some promotion opportunities due to my accent". Abdel's contradictory statements about his experience with accent discrimination might leave one perplexed. However, later in his *testimonio*, he confirms that he has indeed been subjected to accentism. Abdel adds,

> In class, I have some students who comment on the course evaluation saying, "He is teaching a tough course and he is making the course more difficult by his accent". But such comments were from few students. Despite my accent I have won several teaching excellence awards over the years.

Like previous participant immigrants, Abdel proudly identified himself as a hard-working professional. Apparently, he wants to fit in the mainstream American English world but has faced systemic linguistic hurdles, namely accentism. Abdel is not alone. As Malda's case illuminates, other immigrant minority native speakers of English face similar forms of accent discrimination in the United States by individuals from the dominant linguistic group.

Malda's Case

Malda (pseudonym) was born and raised in the Philippines. She immigrated to the United States after she met her husband, a U.S. veteran, who was then stationed in the Philippines. Malda already spoke English as her dominant language before moving to the United States. She stayed home to take care of her son for years while her husband was in the military, before returning to school to pursue a doctorate, which she completed on time. Malda identifies herself as someone who believes in the ideals of the United States, which she claims she loves as the wife of a U.S. military veteran. She talks about the ways she has faced accent discrimination and xenophobia since she has been living here because of her English accent and ethnicity. Malda states:

> My experiences with accent discrimination as an educated woman who came from Southeast Asia and has lived in the United States for 27 years has been challenging. My most recent experience was at Walmart counter where a cashier, upon seeing me and hearing my accent, started the conversation, "I am so impressed that your country really perfected making freeze dried food".

Malda often has to challenge those who have ill-perceived and poorly treated her because of her non-dominant English accent. She did not remain silent when the cashier at Walmart made this insensitive comment about her ethnicity. Malda says she asked, "'Did you mean Japan?' She said 'yes.' I replied, 'But I'm not Japanese.' She said, 'You know what I mean.' At that point, I turned my face and left".

As Malda's counter-narrative indicates, she often has to correct people, in order to get the respect that she deserves–something those who are linguistically privileged do not have to do. Participants' narratives in this unit showed patterns across the data set regarding various forms of accent discrimination they experienced. The following unit explores cases in which participants felt they had not personally experienced accent discrimination but had witnessed close relatives and peers experiencing it, and shared how they were affected by such experiences.

Unit Two

Participants' Testimonios *about Immigrants Facing Accent Discrimination*

Aseya's Case

Aseya (pseudonym) is a 24-year-old female African American undergraduate student who grew up middle-class in the southern United States. Growing up, she witnessed her mother's best friend, an immigrant woman from Egypt, being subjected to discrimination because of her foreign accent. Specifically, as a child, while accompanying her mother's friend to the local supermarket to buy groceries, she witnessed people insulting her because of her accent. Aseya states,

> When I was younger, my mother had an Egyptian friend that was having a hard time adjusting to living in America. My mother would make

me go to the supermarket and other stores with her to help out. I can recall how people would treat me, a nine-year-old, with more respect and kindness than they treated Ms. Hannah because I spoke English without an accent and she had an accent.

Using her mother's friend as a prime example, Aseya unravels the common assumption made about people who speak English in distinct accents. Her narrative points out the extent to which people who speak in non-dominant accents are often assumed to be foreigners and therefore to be feared, while others are perceived as less intelligent than those who speak in standard English accent. Aseya goes on to say,

> My mother's friend would get treated like a low-class citizen because of her Egyptian accent. People would get frustrated because they couldn't understand her; they would yell curses and tell her to go back to her country.

Having an accent does not interfere with one's cognitive or intellectual capabilities. However, Aseya's narrative about her mother's friend seems to suggest that immigrants who speak in non-dominant English accents are looked down upon and treated as unintelligent. Based on the content of her narrative, she seems to have been affected by such experiences. Akayla also witnessed minority immigrants, including bilingual students at her school, being subjected to ridicule because of their accents.

Akayla's Case

Akayla (pseudonym) is a 48-year-old, married Mexican woman. She was born in Mexico and immigrated to the United States with her family when she was a child. She identifies herself as middle-class. She was a middle-school principal pursuing a doctorate in education at the time of the study. Like Aseya, Akayla never felt personally discriminated against because of her accent. However, she witnessed and continues to witness people, including immigrant students and classmates, being discriminated against because of their accents. Akayla states,

> Growing up in Chicago, I found accents to be fascinating. I enjoyed listening to people speak and tried guessing their country of origin. I knew that I, too, had an accent, but I never felt discriminated against because of my accent. When I was in high school, I remember that students who were newcomers were often made fun of when they communicated in class.

Akayla first acknowledges the beauty in diverse accents and then expresses empathy for those who are subject to accent discrimination, saying, "I saw how the students sank into their seats and became withdrawn. I feel bad for the students and knew that aggressors would eventually grow out of their immature behavior". Although she admits that she, too, has an accent, Akayla never feels linguistically mistreated because of it. However, she witnesses immigrant peers facing accent discrimination. Accentism, as Akayla's narrative suggests, is pervasive in schools and has affected the lives of linguistic minorities, including immigrants of color. Akayla is not the only participant who bore witness to accent discrimination occurring. Joanne, a person of color of mixed heritage, also witnessed her mother, an immigrant from the Philippines, being discriminated against because of her accent.

Joanne's Case

Joanne (pseudonym) is a 40-year Filipina-American woman, whose father is a U.S. veteran and mother was an immigrant from the Philippines. She was an assistant school principal when she participated in this study. Like the previous participants, Joanne believed accents are beautiful and stated that she never felt discriminated against because of her accent. However, she witnessed her immigrant mother being humiliated and insulted by strangers for speaking in an accent perceived and treated as "foreign". Joanne states,

> I have witnessed my mother experience accent-based discrimination. She was born in the Philippines, and lived there until she was 21 years old. My father, who was in the U.S. Navy, brought her to the U.S. after they met and married in the Philippines. I witnessed my mother experience accent-discrimination as a young child when people tell her to go back to where she's from upon hearing her speak English.

Joanne's view about accent is that it reflects one's identity and where one is from. Joanne personally never experienced accent discrimination. However, she witnessed her immigrant mother from the Philippine enduring this systemic oppression. Joanne's *testimonio* suggests that those who speak in non-standard accents are routinely linguistically profiled (Baugh, 2018).

Discussion

Depending on where one's accent originates, one may be subject to insidious forms of accent discrimination. In the United States, immigrant minorities are routinely subjected to linguistic discrimination because of their non-standard English accent and related factors, such as ethnicity/race and nationality, in addition to their native language. For example, immigrants, including university professors and college students involved in this study whose English accents differ from the alleged standard American accent, experience accent discrimination in spite of their academic and professional achievements.

Participant's *testimonios* speak to the ways in which they have personally experienced accent discrimination and witnessed family members, classmates, and friends experiencing it, as well; their narratives expose biases about, and discrimination against, non-standard English speakers. Uninformed and biased viewpoints about non-standard accents have influenced the way dominant linguistic groups perceive and treat linguistic minorities, including bilingual college students and professors of color. Participants' *testimonios* also reveal ways in which they have challenged accent discrimination and English-language hegemony.

Moreover, their *testimonios* illustrate how and to what degree accentism has variously affected the lives of linguistic minorities. Even though other study participants, including Akayla and Joanne, have not personally experienced accent discrimination, they witnessed their family members and classmates experiencing it. Akayla and Joanne believe that accents reflect a great deal of linguistic diversity, which American schools and society can benefit from.

Having an identifiable non-dominant accent has added many layers to the identity of linguistically and culturally diverse groups, including study participants. However, it is not speaking with the dominant accent that seems to be the issue; rather, it is people's unfavorable attitude toward noticeable non-dominant accents. Accentism has affected native speakers of English, including African Americans and Latinx people.

Participant's *testimonios* about their experiences with accent discrimination suggest that this systemic oppression is connected to one's native tongue, ethnicity, and country of origin, among other underlying factors. Linguistic protection from accent discrimination seems to be mainly granted to those who are dominant speakers of standard English and from privileged ethnic, racial, and socio-economic backgrounds, as non-standard speakers of English are often treated unfairly linguistically. Their English accents are often seen as deviants from standard English. Abdel's accent, for example, was called "heavy"–a marker particularly associated with immigrant bilingual speakers who speak with a different accent. English accents constructed as "heavy" or "foreign" do not seem to be appreciated in American classrooms and society at large, even though accent in general is a linguistic asset that can contribute, and has contributed, to diversity in American schools and society.

Conclusion

Accent discrimination, which commonly occurs in American schools and other institutions, affects linguistic minorities across language, race, ethnicity, social class, nationality, gender, and sexuality. Those who speak English with an accent have often been denied opportunities, including employment, housing, and job promotion (Baugh, 2018; Lippi-Green, 2012). Very limited opportunities in institutions such as higher education have been given to those who speak English with a noticeably non-standard accent. In universities and colleges, one rarely finds administrators who speak English with an accent occupying key administrative positions, like provost or president. Denying people opportunities because of their accent–something they do not have control over–is really unjust.

Accent discrimination needs to be examined in depth and brought to the forefront of debates on linguistic and educational issues. Just as there are people who are discriminated against because of their race, ethnicity, religion, sexual orientation, gender, disability, and social class, there are those who are subjected to various forms of linguistic discrimination because of their accents. Linguistically marginalized individuals and groups, including the case study participants in this book, are frequently prejudged, made fun of, and denied opportunities because of their non-standard English accent. Despite the multifaceted effects of accentism on linguistic minorities, the right to speak with, and maintain one's accent cannot and should not be denied.

References

Baugh, J. (2000). *Beyond Ebonics: Linguistic Pride and Racial Prejudice*. Oxford: Oxford University Press.

Baugh, J. (2010). *Black Street Speech: Its history, Structure, and Survival*. Texas: University of Texas Press.

Baugh, J. (2018). *Linguistics in Pursuit of Justice*. Cambridge: Cambridge University Press.

Chomsky, N. (2013). *Topics in the Theory of Generative Grammar* (Vol. 56). Berlin, Germany: Walter de Gruyter.

Chomsky, N. (2014). *Aspects of the Theory of Syntax* (Vol. 11). Cambridge, MA: MIT Press.

Labov, W. (2011). *Principles of Linguistic Change, Cognitive and Cultural Factors* (Vol. 3). New York: John Wiley & Sons.

Levy, E. S., & Crowley, C. J. (2012). Policies and Practices Regarding Students with Accents in Speech-Language Pathology Training Programs. *Communication Disorders Quarterly*, 34(1): 59–68.

Lippi-Green, R. (1994). Accent, Standard Language Ideology, and Discriminatory Pretext in the Courts. *Language in Society*, 23(02): 163. doi:10.1017/s0047404500017826.

Lippi-Green, R. (2012). *English with an Accent: Language, Ideology, and Discrimination in the United States*. New York: Routledge.
Livingston, B. A., Schilpzand, P., & Erez, A. (2016). Not What You Expected to Hear. *Journal of Management*, 43(3): 804–833. doi:10.1177/0149206314541151.
Nelson, L. R., Signorella, M. L., & Botti, K. G. (2016). Accent, Gender, and Perceived Competence. *Hispanic Journal of Behavioral Sciences*, 38(2): 166–185. doi:10.1177/0739986316632319.
Nieto, S., & Bode, P. (2018). *Affirming Diversity: The Sociopolitical Context of Multicultural Education* (7th edition). New York: Pearson.

4 Linguistic and Racial Inequities in Higher Education
The Subaltern Speak Out

Approximately 30 years ago, Gayatri Spivak wrote *Can the Subaltern Speak? Reflections on the History of an Idea.* Soon after its release, this widely read essay became a classic (or became canonical). Indeed, it has crossed literary borders, capturing the interest of millions of readers and informing the work of numerous scholars from various fields and across disciplines around the world (Maggio, 2017; Saffari, 2016). *Can the Subaltern Speak?* has sparked many intellectual, educational, and political debates on whether or not the subaltern can speak and who is really considered the subaltern. According to Spivak (2017), the subaltern does speak, contrary to what has been commonly believed. Spivak (2017) states:

> The Subaltern does speak. In that essay the Subaltern spoke but nobody listened. That's why the Subaltern can't speak. For example, the woman who hanged herself actually took good care to make sure that people would know that she was not given over to a unique man and that's not why she was killing herself. But nobody actually remembered that message. So that's why I said the Subaltern cannot speak. Subalterns do indeed resist, not all of them, just as not everyone out of any group is resistant.
>
> (Spivak, as cited in Orelus, 2017, p. 18)

Aligning with Spivak's view, this book in general, and this chapter in particular, argue the subaltern does speak up against social wrongs (Gee, 2011). The subaltern is not always what Fanon (1961) calls "the wretched of the earth". The subaltern can also be working-class people who have managed to become university professors, like participants in the study, who are often perceived and ill-treated. These participants used *testimonios* to denounce linguistic and racial inequities they faced in society at large and in the academy in particular.

DOI: 10.4324/9781315858135-4

Linguistic and Racial Inequities in Higher Education 55

The western academy has historically been a White, monolingual, male-dominated institution. Specifically, from the outset, scholarship and research in western colleges and universities have been dominated by the values of White males, who tend to be monolingual, Christian, able-bodied, and presumably heterosexual (Ahmed, 2012; Tillman, 2001; Turner, 2002, 2003). These males have in fact held the majority of key positions within the academy. Studies document that, in the United States, White males occupy most key administrative university positions, including department chair, dean, provost, and chancellor (Betts et al., 2009; Stanley, 2006). Because of a lack of a fair representation of subaltern professors within these institutions, White males, who tend to be monolingual speakers of English, have by and large taught both White students and linguistic-minority students of color. Consequently, students may not find the opportunity to be taught and mentored by a linguistically and culturally diverse body of faculty who can consistently contribute to their socio-cultural, epistemological, and ontological formation.

The absence of subaltern professors in the western academy might prompt one to ask whether or not the few who are part of this institution have not been strategically utilized to veil a deeper, endemic structure of inequity and exclusion within western institutions at large. This lack of structural inclusion appears to be linked to a lack of genuine effort to diversify the higher-education faculty workforce, exemplified by a failure to integrate qualified subaltern personnel at all levels and across multiple identities, including language, race, ethnicity, sexuality, religion, and nationality. Neither linguistic minority professors nor students of color have been fully integrated into the U.S. academy despite substantial diversity rhetoric. These professors and students have often functioned as "tokens" at elite universities, which formerly were reserved for monolingual White males. Consequently, their identities have been strategically appropriated to conceal serious and persistent linguistic and racial equity, diversity, and inclusion issues.

Because of socio-political movements, namely international student movements in the 1960s, as well as the civil rights, Black, Chicano(a), Native American, queer, and feminist movements, some spaces have been created within the western academy for linguistic and racial minority students and professors. Yet, despite five decades of efforts to diversify American colleges and universities, these institutions remain bastions of White patriarchal dominance. As a consequence, White female faculty, although their White privilege might have enabled many to navigate through more easily and hold higher positions in the academy than subaltern faculty, have yet to occupy key positions of power at a comparable rate as their White male counterparts because of the unequal gendered power relations that persist (Aguirre, 2000).

In other words, whiteness might have helped professional White female faculty and administrators make it through the academic pipeline, but numerically speaking, they still remain part of a subaltern class. As for queer faculty, particularly female queer faculty of color, they are subaltern within subalterns by virtue of the fact that they have to deal not only with sexism, racism, White male elitism, and other isms for being women of color, but also with homophobia because of their sexual orientation (Ahmed, 2012; Kumashiro, 2002). Finally, and equally important, those who speak English with a distinct accent routinely face intersecting forms of oppression, like accentism, in addition to systemic racism and sexism.

The examples highlighted above demonstrate the extent to which these professors experience micro-aggressions and other forms of social and material inequalities at predominantly White institutions. Subaltern professors often refer to being emotionally wounded as a result of systemic violence experienced in the academy over a long period of time, which often leads to deep mental suffering, from which they might not heal.

Regardless of their contribution to the western academy, subaltern professors are often subjected to poor treatment. Such treatment at times comes from students and colleagues who, for example, are unwilling to embrace the diversity of languages, accents, ethnicities, and races, among other identities, that subaltern professors and students bring with them to the academy. As a result, their identities, including their diverse accents, are questioned. In addition to being discriminated against because of their accents, they are also targeted because of ethnicity and race.

This book examines these timely social-justice issues in education, drawing on ideas from sociolinguist and critical race theory frameworks (Baugh, 2018; Delgado Bernal and Villalpando, 2002) and the methodology of *testimonios*. As noted in the previous chapter, this qualitative approach is often employed as a grassroots method for collecting stories that challenge and expose hegemonic inequalities at work in the lives of subaltern populations. The following discussion incorporates *testimonios*—which may be thought of as subaltern stories—collected from subaltern professors and students. Specifically, through these *testimonios*, this book seeks to highlight various ways in which accent and racial discrimination has affected these professors and students in the academy and beyond.

Testimonios as Qualitative Research

As briefly noted in Chapters 2 and 3, historically marginalized groups have used *testimonios* as an alternative, grassroots genre and method to assert their identities and their particular and distinct perceptions of the world.

Testimonios are grounded in people's historical struggles shaping their ontological experiences. Over the last two decades, an increasing number of researchers have drawn on *testimonios* to elucidate serious forms of social injustice experienced by historically oppressed groups, including women, and LGTBQ communities (Anzaldua, 2002a, 2002b). Feminist scholars and researchers, in particular, have drawn on *testimonios* to unveil, analyze, and challenge gender and sexual oppression occurring in schools and in society at large (Anzaldua, 2002a, 2002b; Beverly, 2005; hooks, 2010). Likewise, Latina activist scholars and researchers have used *testimonios* as counter-narratives to talk about Chicanas' daily struggles fighting patriarchy, sexism, homophobia, xenophobia, racism, and other forms of oppression in the academy and society at large (Anzaldua, 2002a; Cantu, 2012; Cruz, 2012; Saavedra and Perez, 2012).

Along the same lines, feminist scholars like Claudia Cervantes-Soon (2012) have conducted qualitative case studies where participants have utilized *testimonios* to talk about the way they and their communities have been ravaged by violence, including violence against young girls and women. Specifically, Cervantes-Soon analyzed *testimonios* by very young Mexican women who have been victims of rape, suicide, incest, and murder in their native land, Mexico, particularly in Cuidad Juarez–a city that has been known as one of the most dangerous cities in the world. Through the *testimonios* of these young women, the various forms and extent of violence they experienced was unveiled. These *testimonios* served as a catalytic tool to articulate how and to what degree the violence occurring in Juarez affected their daily lives and those of their families. Cervantes-Soon (2012) states,

> These *testimonios* shed light on the life experiences and identity formation of young women coming of age in the south of the border and reveal the knowledge and wisdom they have gained in their struggle for freedom, dignity, and life. They also expose the epistemological and pedagogical nature of young women's discourse and wisdom characterized by testimonios as counter-narratives, confessions, and consejos.
>
> (p. 373)

Subaltern groups have used *testimonios* as counter-stories to talk about and resist systemic oppression. But it is important to note that *testimonios* have equally been used to chronicle the joy and happiness of celebrating life (Cruz, 2012; Delgado Bernal, 2008, 2009; Delgado Bernal and Villalpando, 2002; Flores Carmona and Delgado Bernal, 2012). In the context of higher education, subaltern researchers have used *testimonios* to voice challenges to the hegemonic patriarchal, racist, and elitist nature of the western academy (hooks, 2010; Prieto and Villenas, 2012; Smith, 1999). Many subaltern professors have been historically *ethnicitized* in the academy, as their ethnicity, languages, and accents are often stigmatized, targeted, and pushed to the margins.

The Indigenous knowledge that subaltern researchers bring with them and the various methods they use to affirm their presence in the academy are often overlooked and labeled as "too subjective" (Darder, 2011; Grande, 2015). This approach privileges objectivity, which is seen as the epitome of western academic culture. As a consequence, the use of *testimonios* and other ways of knowing are often not respected or legitimated in the academic world. Yet, as shown by this book, *testimonios* have enabled people to reflect on, analyze, and unveil social and material practices of inequalities experienced in the academy and the society at large.

Data

Data for this chapter consists of six *testimonios* selected from the set. As already noted, minority professors and students involved in this book are from various countries and linguistic, cultural, and ethnic backgrounds. While some are U.S.-born, others are from Latin America, the Philippines, India, Jordan, and Spain; they speak different native languages and use English as the lingua franca to communicate, teach, and conduct research at various universities across the U.S. Their *testimonios* are intergenerational, as they are at different stages in their academic and professional journeys. While some are emerita and emeritus full professors, others are students or assistant and associate professors, demonstrating that subaltern groups have experienced linguistic and racial inequities at different stages and levels in their career. Their *testimonios* are analyzed in this chapter as well so as to show patterns across the data set about various forms of accent discrimination as well as racial oppression that subaltern professors, students, and other professionals have experienced in American society particularly and the Western academy as a whole.

Living to Tell Their Own Story

Part I: Accent Discrimination Cases

In the western academy, in addition to facing class, gender, and race inequities, subaltern professors and students are both routinely subjected to various forms of accent discrimination. They come from diverse linguistic, racial, and socio-economic backgrounds and speak English with different accents. They are victims of accent discrimination, for their accent is often arbitrarily linked to their ethnicity, race, and country of origin, among other factors.

Testimonio of Participant 1

Naomi (pseudonym) was in her mid-60s and originally from Columbia. She was a full professor with decades of teaching experience in both her native land and the United States, where she had taught students from various backgrounds for over 20 years before retiring. She defines herself as a scholar activist. She is known to bring social justice issues to the fore of educational and political debates locally, nationally, and internationally. In her *testimonio*, Naomi exposes and challenges insensitive comments students and other individuals made about her English accent. Naomi narrates:

> Discrimination/ignoring or complaining because of my accent in English is a regular experience, although it has become less frequent. I guess because I have developed a less 'heavy' accent. For instance, at stores I have been ignored, or they have offered to call a person who "speaks Spanish" to 'help' me. As I speak, students or other people noticeably go deaf or complain that they do not understand me because of my 'accent'. After 15+ years teaching at the university level in the US, I have developed strategies to augment my speaking with ways to visualize or read in addition to listening to what I say. There are still students who complain in code about my accent. The latest anonymous comment to the question, "How can this course be improved?" "Having an instructor I can understand when they [sic] are talking".

Testimonio of Participant 2

Jose (pseudonym) is from Puerto Rico and moved to the United States to pursue graduate studies immediately after completing his bachelors' degree. He is currently a history professor specializing in Caribbean history. Jose is known to be a prolific writer. He is now in his 40s and married with children. Jose says:

> Accent discrimination in my professional life has come in several ways. It was widespread among fellow graduate students when I first arrived to the U.S. and started an M.A. program in history at Temple

University. Some of my classmates just didn't have the patience to listen to me and zone-out every time I presented or commented in class during my first year in that program. It took me a while to get the handle of it and I used to get incredibly embarrassed by it to the point that I spoke as little as possible in class. But I worked on my "accent" and practiced words that were hard to pronounce before going to class . . . .. Finally, though the hundreds of students I had in Rutgers and UMass never complained about my accent, one semester at Marist College (New York), in a particularly difficult section, some five students, aware that they were failing the class, banded together and in their class evaluation wrote that to improve the class they should "hire an American who spoke English to teach it" and several variations of that comment. I suspect that had something to do with not having my contract renewed next year. Awareness of how some people react to my "accent" in English has led me to do a few things in professional settings: I speak loudly using a commanding voice and looking people in the face, and I dress more professionally than my native English-speaker colleagues as a way to command respect. Nowadays, I'm much more comfortable with my accent so at the beginning of a class or presentation I sometimes fake the thickest of accents, let my audience or class be horrified for a few seconds and then I speak in a pretty "standard", easy-to-understand English.

Testimonio *of Participant 3*

Manz (pseudonym), a subaltern professor in her 50s, is originally from Jordan, where her parents and other relatives still live. She identifies as queer, and has been with her partner for over a decade. She is an activist scholar, and her research focuses on the identity of Muslim girls. Specifically, Manz's research focuses on normative discourses shaping Muslim girls' bodily experiences. Her research is guided by a commitment to work with Muslim girls, to challenge and interrupt any of the hegemonizing discourses in their lives, and to find *with* them more democratic and equitable learning opportunities. In the following *testimonio*, she narrates an incident in which she felt she was discriminated against because of her non-dominant accent, while her Canadian-British partner's accent was glorified. Manz states:

> I have been in several situations in which my accent did not work in advantage, or I was somehow disrespected. However, it has not been more obvious than lately when accompanied by my partner. She is Canadian of British origin, and her accent is picked up right the way

and almost complimented for. Recently, we went to buy a product from BestBuy here in Las Cruces, NM, USA. I am the tech savvy person in the family. As soon as I started to speak to the salesperson, he began to repeat some of my phrases as if to confirm their accuracy. Once he heard my partner spoke, he turned towards her and diagnosed me, to continue explaining, discussing the pros of the product we are asking about. He immediately praised her accent and told her it is beautiful and wishes he could speak to her.

Discussion

Like Naomi and Jose, Manz states that she personally experiences accent hegemony because of her Jordanian-accented English, whereas her partner, who is Canadian of British origin, was praised for her British accent. Manz was ignored and looked down upon, while her partner received assistance without requesting it by virtue of the fact that she speaks with a British accent, and she is White. Like Naomi and Jose, she indicates that speaking in a discernable accent adds another layer to her linguistic identity. Situating the accent issue in a linguistic, racial, and political context, it can be argued that these participants' accents most likely would not be a problem if they were White, middle-class Americans or Europeans, especially from northern or western Europe.

Some accents are considered well-bred and high-class, while others are considered low- class. The social construction of the standard British and American English accents places it on a sociolinguistic pedestal at the expense of other English accents perceived and treated as nonstandard. This accent bias is clearly visible in today's American political climate and culture. For example, the former First Lady, Melania Trump, delivered a keynote speech at the American Republican Convention in July 2016, and no political analysts made insensitive comments about her distinct English accent.

Likewise, Arnold Schwarzenegger, the former governor of California, who speaks English in a distinct accent, was once touted as a potential presidential candidate despite his ineligibility as an Austrian-born immigrant. Neither the former First Lady nor the former governor have been discriminated against and marginalized because of their accent, unlike bilingual students and professors participating in this study. This is to point out that the accent issue needs to be linked to race, social class, and country of origin.

Like any form of discrimination, accent discrimination is a serious matter. Linguistic minorities are often subjected to various forms of accent discrimination limiting their professional life chances and opportunities. They are frequently prejudged, scrutinized, doubted, and denied opportunities because of their non-standard way of expressing themselves in English. Accounts of individuals who have been subjected to discrimination and other forms of discrimination need to be taken more seriously for fairness, equity, and inclusion purposes. The next section analyzes *testimonios* of three subaltern professors experiencing race, accent, and language hegemony in higher education and society at large.

Part Two: **Testimonios** *on Racial and Gender Inequities*

Like accent discrimination, race and gender inequities constitute some of the challenges that subaltern professors face in the western academy. As previously noted, many subaltern professors are from marginalized backgrounds and have used resources made available to them along the way to study and become university professors. However, such status does not guarantee them the same protection and representation in the western academy as their privileged White counterparts. Consequently, as the following *testimonios* suggest, they often have to fight isolation, marginalization, and micro-aggressions that they routinely face in the academy.

Testimonio *of Participant 4*

Freda (pseudonym) is a subaltern retired professor in her 70s, originally from Puerto Rico. Freda is an internationally recognized Freirian scholar. She is Professor Emerita at the University of Illinois Urbana Champaign and, before retiring, held the Leavey Presidential Chair of Ethics and Moral Leadership at Loyola Marymount University in Los Angeles.. Her scholarship critically focuses on social inequalities within schools and society. What follows is Freda's *testimonio*:

> My experience in the academy has truthfully, for the most part, been a nightmare! It has been extremely difficult because, as I came to realize, I entered academia with very different cultural, class, gendered, and political sensibilities. More importantly, I had no real preparation with respect to the professional culture of academia. I didn't come from a family of people who were formally educated. The way people construct popular discourse in the barrio in comparison to the culture of higher education is very different. Even now, I seem to possess a very different ideological position than most of my colleagues, including many on the Left. Moreover, I have a very clear commitment to a larger political project that requires connection with communities. My work isn't about a career, so all of this is very disconcerting for those who benefit from the system, irrespective of their espoused political

leanings. In a lot of ways, I have felt like I am seen a bit like a traitor, a disenfranchised person who was allowed entry into the ivory halls, but who can't be trusted to protect the privilege or conserve allegiance to the institution. There has been an unspoken expectation that I should abandon my collective political commitment in favor of an individual focus on my scholarship, primarily as an extension and resource for the university. But since I have been simply unwilling to do so, I have known much isolation and marginalization as a consequence. Moreover, I realize that, as a working-class woman of color, I was never expected to enter into academia and be successful.

Testimonio *of Participant 5*

Veranda (pseudonym) is an Asian female professor in her 50s, born and raised in India. She moved to the United States to pursue graduate studies. After the completion of her doctoral work, she was hired at a state university in Massachusetts, where she has been teaching and doing research for over two decades. She is known for her activist work dedicated to defending women's and workers' rights in particular, and human rights in general, in both her native India and the United States. Her *testimonio* exposes various forms of systemic challenges, including xenophobia, sexism, and racism, that foreign-born subaltern professors face in the western academy. Veranda states:

> For me, it's been a learning curve, a very steep learning curve. There's a whole liberal discourse around multiculturalism, diversity, affirmative action, and the importance of having faculty of color at universities. When you enter these institutions, you realize that there's so little in terms of actual recognition, appreciation, and respect for faculty of color and for diversity. As a new assistant professor, I remember American students in the program expected me to teach a course on yoga! You are a token, and they'd like you to stay that way. There are exceptions of course, individual colleagues who don't fall in this category, but for the most part, the entire culture of the institution, departments as a whole would rather you operate as a token, and not bring yourself, your questions, your critique into the academic space. When I came in, I found that there's this constant pressure to prove oneself over and over again. There's constant questioning of one's capabilities, competency, and contribution. And also, because I think one's particular kind of political commitments to Third World people and their struggles— this directs my work very differently. So, the work has to emerge from the issues and questions that are coming up in those regions, from the

people's struggles in particular places rather than from what funding is available at the moment or what the USAID or World Bank is interested in funding at this point.

Testimonio *of Participant 6*

Praviaj (pseudonym) was born into a middle-class family in India, and immigrated to the United States to continue his studies. He chaired the history department at a university in New England. His research focuses on international political affairs, including the Middle East. He identifies himself as a Marxist intellectual. He is married with children. In talking about his experience as a minority professor in the western academy, Praviaj states,

> My experience has been good partly because I have been a part of the vaunted model minority, which I have written a lot about. Asians were barred from entering the United States from 1924 to 1965. During this very long period of about 41 years, no Asians could come in legally. Some came in as professors. But typically, there was no mass migration. In 1965 Asians were finally allowed to enter the United States again. This was at the same time as the civil rights movement had its major victory with the Civil Rights Act and the Voting Rights Act. Asians became part of the ideological reconfiguration of racism. The idea that was put out culturally was to look at these Asians as making it. The questions that have arisen from this were: The Indians are so smart, why do Black people, why do Hispanic people need welfare? Why do they need state support? Why can't they be like the model minority? So, in that sense Indian people had to suffer some forms of discrimination while at the same time enjoyed the fruits of being treated as a model minority. Now, the model minority is a bogus narrative, because after all we were not brought in on slave ships. We were chosen, that is, people with high advanced degrees were chosen to come into the U.S. So, to compare a state-selected population with a randomly selected population that was captured and brought to the country is incredibly disingenuous. The model minority thesis is a garbage thesis. But that doesn't mean it doesn't have real effects. The real effect it has had on me is that people look at me and say, "you are Indian, you are safe, you work hard, and you are smart". So, in that sense I have not had an adverse experience in the American Academy. Now I've had an adverse experience in that I see how other colleagues are treated, and that gives me pain. But I don't want to collapse my experience with everybody of color because I think that's also disingenuous.

Discussion

Subaltern professors' accent, race/ethnicity, and gender, among other factors, place them in distinct social brackets, and influence the way people idiosyncratically perceive and treat them in the academy and society at large. Despite their differences, subaltern professors are all affected by institutional accentism, racism, xenophobia, and sexism, albeit in varying manner and degree

As Praviaj's *testimonio* illuminates, his life and professional experiences in the U.S. academy and society have been different because of specific stereotypes attached to Indians in general. In Praviaj's words, Asians generally tend to be seen through a rather positive lens compared to African Americans and other Blacks.

While some subaltern professors seem to be more concerned about race, language, and accent issues in particular–as they might be subjected to these forms of oppression more frequently than others–other scholars, like Freda and Veranda, appear to be as concerned about sexism, classism, patriarchy, and elitism in the academy as about racism. Specifically, because of their backgrounds and experiences, these female professors of color seem concerned equally about sexism and racism, whereas their male colleagues of color seem to focus exclusively on racism and White supremacy.

Subaltern professors' backgrounds, encompassing their gender, race, social class, and nationality, among other characteristics, place them in homogenous brackets. However, as acknowledged earlier, regardless of their identities and other characteristics differentiating them from one another, they are all victims of micro-aggressions, although they might not be affected to the same degree as their life and professional experiences are shaped by different socio-economic, ethnic, gender, and cultural realities, among others.

All forms of oppression intersect, and thus they all need to be challenged together. The personal and professional backgrounds of subaltern professors are very complex. They are one and many at the same time–they are diversity in unity. That is, they might be shaped by similar historical experiences and memories of systemic oppression.

In addition to racial, gender, and class oppression professors of color face in the academy, they face linguistic form of discrimination to which subaltern professors speaking English in distinct accent are frequently subjected. As prime examples, immigrant professors of color who speak English in distinct accents are subjected to linguicism and xenophobia, in addition to institutional racism. Like many subaltern professors, their intelligence and qualification are often questioned because of their accent.

Conclusion

Subaltern professors have been subjected to multiple forms of marginalization in the academy. Their *testimonios* highlight how and to what extent various kinds of oppression intersect to affect them. Subaltern professors speaking English in a distinct accent often experience accent discrimination, but such discrimination has not yet been fully documented. Likewise, female faculty experience gender inequality, while those who are queer and immigrants of color face intersectional forms of oppression. People from privileged positions in society might not fully comprehend what it is like to be discriminated against because of one's identity, whether it be race-, gender-, accent-, language-, sexuality-, or religion-based identity. However, as Freda's and Veranda's *testimonios* seem to imply, for people placed in subaltern positions, facing and resisting systemic oppression has been their reality even before entering the academy.

As this book shows, the western academy has a racist and sexist linguistic culture that affects subaltern professors in ways that are often unseen and disguised. Their voices ought to be heard. They deserve to be respected, recognized, and genuinely included in the academy. At the same time, however, the *testimonios* of the participants, including those of the university professors, should not be used to generalize about all linguistically and racially minoritized groups, as the experience of each person is different and unique–we all come from different walks of linguistic and ethnic life, despite the common struggle that unites us. Rather, their *testimonios* should serve as a dialogical entry point to contextualize and examine the experiences of linguistically marginalized groups fighting accentism,, xenophobia, racism, sexism, and White male dominance.

References

Aguirre, A. (2000). *Women and Minority Faculty in the Academic Workplace: Recruitment, Retention, and Academic Culture*. San Francisco: Jossey-Bass.

Ahmed, S. (2012). *On Being Included: Racism and Diversity in Institutional Life*. NC: Duke University Press Books.

Anzaldua, G. (2002a). Now Let Us Shift . . . The Path of Conocimiento . . . Inner Work, Public Acts. In G. Anzaldua & A. Keating (Eds.), *This Bridge We Call Home: Radical Visions for Transformation* (pp. 540–578). New York, NY: Routledge.

Anzaldua, G. (2002b). Preface. In G. Anzaldua & A. Keating (Eds.), *This Bridge We Call Home: Radical Visions for Transformation* (pp. 1–5). New York, NY: Routledge.

Baugh, J. (2018). *Linguistics in pursuit of justice*. Cambridge, England: Cambridge University Press.

Betts, K., Urias, D., Chavez, J., & Betts, K. (2009). Higher Education and Shifting U.S. Demographics: Need for Visible Administrative Career Paths, Professional

Development, Succession Planning & Commitment to Diversity. Retrieved on 06/12/2017 www.academicleadership.org/emprical_research/623_printer.shtml.

Beverly, J. (2005). Testimonio, Subalternity, and Narrative Authority. In N. K. Denzin & Y. S. Lincoln (Eds.), *Handbook of Qualitative Research* (pp. 555–565). Thousand Oaks, CA: Sage.

Cantu, N. (2012). Getting There Cuando No Hay Camino (When There is No Path): Paths to Discovery Testimonios by Chicanas in Stem. *Equity & Excellence in Education*, 45(3): 472–487.

Cervantes-Soon, C. (2012). Testimonios of Life and Learning in the Borderlands: Subaltern Juarez Girls Speak. *Equity & Excellence in Education*, 45(3): 373–391.

Cruz, C. (2012). Making Curriculum from Scratch: Testimonio in an Urban Classroom. *Equity & Excellence in Education*, 45(3): 460–471.

Darder, A. (2011). *A Dissident Voice: Essays on Culture, Pedagogy and Power*. New York: Peter Lang.

Delgado Bernal, D. (2008). La trenza de identidades: Weaving Together My Personal, Professional, and Communal Identities. In K. P. Gonzalez & R. V. Padilla (Eds.), *Doing the Public Good: Latina/o Scholars Engage Civic Participation* (pp. 134–148). Sterling, VA: Stylus.

Delgado Bernal, D. (2009). Introduction: Our Testimonios as Methodology, Pedagogy, and a Messy Work in Progress. In S. Aleman, D. Delgado Bernal, J. Flores Carmona, L. Galas, & M. Garza (Eds.), *Unidas We Heal: Testimonios of Mind/Body/Soul. Latinas Telling Testimonios* (pp. 4–6). Salt Lake City, UT: University of Utah. [Edited in-house book].

Delgado Bernal, D., & Villalpando, O. (2002). An Apartheid of Knowledge in Academia: The Struggle Over the "Legitimate" Knowledge of Faculty of Color. *Equity and Excellence in Education*, 35: 169–180.

Fanon, Frantz. (1961). "The Wretched of the Earth". *Trans. Richard Philcox*. New York: Grove Press 6 (2004).

Flores Carmona, J., & Delgado Bernal, D. (2012). Oral Histories in the Classroom: Home and Community Pedagogies. In C. E. Sleeter & E. Soriano Ayala (Eds.), *Building Solidarity between Schools and Marginalized Communities: International Perspectives*. New York: Teachers College Press.

Gee, J. (2011). *How to do Discourse Analysis. A Tool Kit*. New York: Routledge.

Grande, S. (2015, September 28). *Red Pedagogy: Native American Social and Political Thought* (10th edition). Lanham, MD: Rowman & Littlefield Publishers.

hooks, b. (2010). *Teaching Critical Thinking: Practical Wisdom*. New York, NY: Taylor & Francis.

Kumashiro, K. (2002). *Troubling Education: Troubling Education: Queer Activism and Anti-Oppressive Pedagogy*. New York: Routledge.

Lemke, J. L. (2002). Travels in Hypermodality. *Visual Communication*, 1(30): 299–325.

Maggio, S. (2017). "Can the Subaltern Be Heard?": Political Theory, Translation, Representation, and Gayatri Chakravorty. *Alternatives*, 32(2007): 419–443.

Orelus, P. W. (2017). *Social Justice for the Oppressed: Critical Educators and Public Intellectuals Speak Out*. Lanham, MD: Rowman & Littlefield Publisher.

Prieto, L., & Villenas, S. (2012). Pedagogies from Nepantla: Testimonio, Chicana/Latina Feminisms and Teacher Classrooms. *Equity & Excellence in Education*, 45(3): 411–429.

Rodriguez, J. C., & Reyes, K. B. (2012). Testimonio: Origins, Terms, and Resources. *Equity & Excellence in Education*, 45(3): 525–538.

Saavedra, C., & Perez, M. S. (2012). Chicana and Black Feminisms: Testimonies of Theory, Identity, and Multiculturalism. *Equity & Excellence in Education*, 45(3): 430–443.

Saffari, S. (2016). Can the Subaltern be Heard? Knowledge Production, Representation, and Responsibility in International Development. *Transcience*, 7(1).

Stanley, C. A. (Ed.). (2006). *Faculty of Color: Teaching in Predominantly White Colleges and Universities*. Bolton, MA: Anker.

Tillman, L. C. (2001). Mentoring African American Faculty in Predominantly White Institutions. *Research in Higher Education*, 42: 295–325.

Turner, C. (2002). Women of Color in Academe. *Journal of Higher Education*, 73: 74–93.

Turner, C. (2003). Incorporation and Marginalization in the Academy: From Border Toward Center for Faculty of Color? *Journal of Black Studies*, 34: 112–125.

5 In Pursuit of Linguistic Equity, Diversity, and Inclusion

Equity, diversity, and inclusion often emerge in discussions of/concerning... race and gender issues. These embedded social justice words are also evoked in conversations about sexuality, ability, and age. However, rarely, if ever, does accent equity, diversity, and inclusion take center stage in heated political debates, even though this is an issue that should concern everyone, given its importance in our day-to-day life. We communicate every day with an accent, regardless of the language we speak. To expand on the arguments made in the previous chapters, this chapter examines/analyzes/interrogates... participants' narratives as a point of reference to expose the effects of accent discrimination on minoritized linguistic groups, while at the same time underscoring the importance of accent equity, diversity, and inclusion (EDI).

Participants' narratives help us understand the root causes and effects of accent discrimination on linguistic minorities. That is, their narratives reveal various contexts, different ways, and the extent to which they received ill treatment in schools and society at large because of their accent. Accent discrimination hurts, and this fact needs to be part of discussions of equity, diversity, and inclusion issues. Accent discrimination also needs to be studied in conjunction with systemic forms of oppression, like racism, xenophobia, and classism, because people who are often discriminated against because of their accent tend to be members of racially, socioeconomically, and linguistically marginalized groups, including immigrants from developing countries.

By contrast, those who are speakers of standard English, particularly monolingual White Americans and Europeans, are less likely to be discriminated against because of their accent. For instance, Henry Kissinger's and Arnold Schwarzenegger's Whiteness, social class, and geographical location might have saved them from public ridicule because of their accented English. The mainstream media have not made any negative comments

DOI: 10.4324/9781315858135-5

about the accent of these two high-profile White male individuals. However, Jesse Jackson was made fun of when he was running for president because of his accent. Specifically, Reverend Jackson's accent was ridiculed supposedly for being unclear and unintelligent (Lippi-Green, 2012). He was accused of speaking Ebonics, as if it is a crime to speak one's language. African Americans in general, and those who speak Ebonics in particular, are routinely and unfairly discriminated against because of their accent.

People who are subjected to accent discrimination are often oppressed linguistic groups, including both immigrants and domestic linguistic minorities, like African Americans, Native Americans, Latinx, and Asians. These groups are often told that they have to learn proper English so they can become part of the White mainstream and the global English community. Yet, the same group of people who told them that they needed to learn English would be the ones later discriminating against them for speaking English with an accent.

As the narrative of Mary, the immigrant participant from Jamaica, illustrates, immigrants are often told as soon as they arrive in the United States that they have to learn standard English if they want to be part of the American mainstream society. The irony is that many have learned English and have tried to assimilate in the American White mainstream culture only to be reminded constantly, through xenophobic and racist comments coming from linguistically insensitive individuals, that they do not belong here because of their English accents.

Similarly, domestic linguistic minorities, including those from immigrant families, are also discriminated against because of their accent. For example, Maria was complimented for "speaking English so well without an accent", even though she was born and raised in the United States. Other domestic minorities, like Jen, who is African American and has been speaking English all her life, have been discriminated against because of their accent.

Since their ancestors were forcibly taken from the continent of Africa to be exported as commodities to the Americas, African Americans have been living in the United States for generations speaking English. Yet many of them have been discriminated against for speaking African American Vernacular English–a dialect of English richly rooted in their history and culture, deviating from the so-called standard American English (Baugh, 2018; Nieto & Bode, 2018). Likewise, Native Americans were forcibly taken from their families to be educated in White Anglo boarding schools, where they were stripped of their native languages and accents, culture, and family ties. In short, they were forcibly Anglicized and Europeanized.

Toward Accent Equity, Diversity, and Inclusion

All accents deserve equal respect, for they reflect people's identity. Just as people should not be discriminated against because of their race, gender, and sexuality, they should not be subjected to personal humiliation because of their accent. Discriminating against someone or a group of people because of their accent is nothing but an assault on their identity.

People do not have any control over what languages and accents they were born into and grew up speaking. Adult second-language learners, for example, do not have any control over their non-native accents. People learn a second, third, or fourth language to expand their linguistic repertoire, including by being able to connect with others from various linguistic and cultural backgrounds. Therefore, they should not be punished for their accents, particularly when, in fact, all of us speak with an accent. How diverse would the world be, if there were only one language and one type of accent, and one category of people living in it? In other words, if we were living in a monolingual world occupied by people of the same race and culture and who speak with the same language in the same accent, what kind of world would that be? Would we be able to talk about linguistic diversity?

Stated otherwise, how can we honestly talk about diversity when people who speak English with a non-dominant or nonstandard accent have been discriminated against at school, work, and other places? How can we truthfully talk about EDI when people who hold key positions in American society tend to be monolingual White males? In order to have an equitable, diverse, and inclusive society, a profound shift in the linguistic paradigm needs to happen institutionally. More specifically, institutions such as schools, the mainstream media, and the workplace need to create space for competent bilingual and multilingual individuals to hold key and influential positions, such as president, provost, dean, department chair, director, news broadcaster, and CEO, among others.

For example, in the U.S. media, particularly the U.S. mainstream media, rarely have we ever seen news broadcasters or reporters speaking with a non-dominant English accent. When someone with an accent is featured in the U.S. mainstream media, such as on Disney television shows, he or she is often subject to ridicule. For example, in the popular Disney television show, *Ant Farm and Jessie*, they portray a South Asian boy supposedly adopted by some American family imitating a South Asian accent, and an African American girl who, in some episodes, tries to imitate a Caribbean type of accent only to entertain the audience that laughs at such accents.

Moreover, at major U.S. universities, rarely do we have university presidents, provosts, or vice-provosts with a recognized non-dominant English accent. It is usually monolingual English speakers, particularly White males, who hold these key positions. Yet the word "diversity" has been used on the website of these institutions for advertisement. When would the word be translated into reality at these institutions? That is, when would such a word cease to be used superficially? Ahmed (2010) observes:

> Again, the suggestion here is that the appeal of diversity is about looking and feeling good, as an orientation that obscures inequalities, like the obscuring of a rotten core behind a shiny surface. As such, diversity as a term has a marketing appeal; it allows the University to sell itself, by presenting itself as a happy place, a place where differences are celebrated, welcomed, and enjoyed. Diversity becomes a brand, and a form of organizational pride. Not only does this re-branding of the university as being diverse work to conceal racism, but it also works to re-imagine the university as being anti-racist and even beyond race: as if the colours of different races have "integrated" to create a new hybrid or even bronzed face.
>
> (Cited in Mirza and Joseph, p, 144)

Historically, in the United States there have been many movements, such as the civil rights movement, the women's movement, and the LBTQ movement, among others, that have fought against institutional racism, sexism, and homophobia, and for equality and social justice on behalf of the oppressed. Likewise, there should be a grassroots movement specifically aimed at battling accentism. Accent discrimination is a linguistic oppression that seems to have gone unnoticed in the public eyes.

Very few scholars have specifically examined accent discrimination in their scholarly work,. Speaking with a non-dominant accent is often associated with a lack of intelligence and being foreign (Baugh, 2018; Lippi-Green, 2012). These stigmas affect students' self-esteem and can preclude them from succeeding academically. It is painful to live in a multilingual society, like the United States, where people continue to be discriminated against because of their diverse English accents. It is time to create larger democratic spaces for people with all accents to be part of American society.

How can a country be called democratic and land of the free when linguistic minorities, including minoritized students, professors, and other individuals, have been mistreated as second-class citizens, and have been specifically discriminated against because of their accents? These questions are worth asking and further exploring, as doing so might help us to understand linguistic disparity and its implications for learning and for the identities of linguistically marginalized groups living in the United States. The final chapter explores linguistic discrimination in the non-U.S. context of colonized lands.

References

Baugh, J. (2018). *Linguistics in Pursuit of Justice*. Cambridge: Cambridge University Press.

Chomsky, N. (2014). *Aspects of the Theory of Syntax* (Vol. 11). Cambridge, MA: MIT Press.

Lippi-Green, R. (2012). *English with an Accent: Language, Ideology and Discrimination in the United States* (2nd edition). New York: Routledge.

Nieto, S., & Bode, P. (2018). *Affirming Diversity: The Sociopolitical Context of Multicultural Education* (7th edition). New York: Pearson.

Phillipson, R. (1992). *Linguistic Imperialism*. Oxford, England: Oxford University Press.

6 Exposing the Effects of Linguoelitism on Linguistic Minorities

Like other forms of systemic oppression, linguoelitism, which is intrinsically connected to accentism, has tremendously affected linguistically disfranchised communities, including multilingual students and professionals. Linguoelitism is a dominant linguistic ideology that privileges socially constructed standard languages and accents over others that are portrayed and treated as subaltern. Like accentism, it is linked to the interwoven factors of power, class, race, and nationality. Because of linguoelitism, groups from historically marginalized backgrounds are routinely subjected to linguistic discrimination for speaking in accents constructed and treated as substandard (Gluszek and Dovidio, 2010; Neuliep and Speten-Hansen, 2013; Skutnabb-Kangas and Dunbar, 2010).

Linguoelitism primarily affects linguistic minorities from marginalized backgrounds, including bilingual and multilingual immigrants speaking English and other languages, like French, in accents deviating from the alleged standard accent. Indeed, people from marginalized linguistic, socioeconomic, and racial backgrounds are regularly subjected to linguoelitism because of their distinct accents or dialects (Ahmed et al., 2013; Kinzler and DeJesus, 2013; Lippi-Green, 2012). Sociologists and linguists alike have explored linkages between language, class, race, and power (see Baugh, 2010; Bourdieu, 1999; Gee, 2011; Labov, 2011; Pennycook, 2017; Phillipson, 2009). For example, Bourdieu (1999) examines the way in which both language and class influence social interaction between middle-class and working-class students. The late French sociologist also analyzes how class informs people's modes of expression, behavior, styles, and taste. Linguistically insensitive individuals from the dominant class often discriminate against those speaking non-dominant languages and/or speaking in accents labelled as "gibberish". Bourdieu (1999, p. 49) states,

> The code, in the sense of cipher, that governs written language, which is identified with correct language, as opposed to the implicitly inferior

DOI: 10.4324/9781315858135-6

conversational language, acquires the force of law in and through the educational system. The educational system, whose scale of operations grew in extent and intensity throughout the nineteenth century, no doubt directly helped to devaluate popular modes of expression, dismissing them as "slang" and "gibberish" and to impose recognition of the legitimate language.

Bourdieu's (1999) statement suggests that linguistic domination and class disparity are manifested in various forms in schools, impacting the learning of students, particularly those from working-class backgrounds. Like Bourdieu, linguists and sociolinguists unpack privileges associated with standard language and accents (See Gee, 2004, 2011; Labov, 2011; Phillipson, 2009; Smith, 2017). For example, Gee (2011) argues that the discourse that middle-class students, particularly White middle-class students, are apprenticed into at home is usually similar, if not identical, to the one valued in mainstream classrooms, putting them in a more advantageous academic position than their poor, working-class student counterparts, who might not have been exposed to such a discourse.

Similarly, Smith (2017) examines the social construction of standard British accents and unpacks privileges attributed to such accents. She suggests that the middle-class discourse that affluent British and U.S. students bring with them to school better positions them than linguistic minorities, namely working-class British and U.S. counterparts, who might not be apprenticed into such discourse. She documents the ways in which linguistic stratification influences asymmetrical power relations between privileged students and those whose accents and dialects have been relegated to the margins.

In the United States, standard American English is highly praised and desired, whereas people whose accents deviate from this standard often face linguistic discrimination. African Americans speaking Ebonics are cases in point noted earlier. Specifically, members of this linguistic minority group are routinely subjected to accent discrimination for speaking African American Vernacular English (AAVE), which is seen as "lower" than standard American English. Indeed, African Americans have historically been subject to linguistic profiling for speaking in dialects or accents that are socially constructed as lower standard (Baugh, 1999, 2010).

Like African Americans, linguistic minority immigrants, including those from Latin America, similarly face discriminatory linguistic mistreatment in the United States because of their native tongue and English accent (Lippi-Green, 2012). Indeed, in the United States, linguistic disparity between standard American English and minority languages is pervasive. Baugh (2010), Labov (2011), and other linguists unravel how linguistic and racial stratification has affected linguistic minorities, particularly African

Americans speaking Ebonics. Baugh (1999, 2010) points out ways in which African American speech patterns are different from those of their White counterparts, particularly from middle-class backgrounds:

> Despite all that linguistics has been able to teach us, however, black English continues to stigmatize speakers as "uneducated" members of society. The persistence of AAVE and the misconceptions about it pose a challenge to our society. Should some citizens be discriminated against because of our collective linguistic ignorance?
>
> (Baugh, 1999, p. 6)

There are linguistic flaws inherent in the social construction of standard English. Like standard English, Black English is rule-governed and connected to the historical and cultural heritage of African Americans from slavery onwards. Baugh carefully demonstrates the ways in which Black English is embedded in African American music, religious practices, cultural traditions, and beliefs. Yet, AAVE and other minority languages continue to be seen as inferior.

Standard American and British Englishes have been promoted through the English-only movement in the United States and the English Language Teaching program in the U.K. (Macedo et al., 2015; Phillipson, 1992). These programs and movements are part of western neoliberal and neocolonial projects designed to promote American and British standard English and culture abroad, often at the expense of other languages and cultures—a form of linguistic domination Phillipson (1992) cogently calls "linguistic imperialism".

Despite its global dominance, English is not the only Western language that has had a hegemonic influence on other languages and peoples around the globe. French has also had a tremendous influence on neo-colonized countries and people around the world. Language hegemony has had serious effects on linguistic minorities. As previously noted in the first chapter, in Haiti, such hegemony primarily affects disenfranchised Haitians speaking Creole (Degraff, 2001, 2018, 2019). This closing chapter draws from data collected over the course of a year to analyze the ways in which linguoelitism, analyzed here as twin sister of accentism, has affected disenfranchised groups not only in the western world but also in the Caribbean where, for example, working-class Haitians have been subjected to French language and accent hegemony.

Context

Jacmel is the city in Haiti where I spent a sabbatical year collecting field notes for a larger, longitudinal, qualitative research project on language and

Exposing the Effects of Linguoelitism on Linguistic Minorities 77

regional accents, from which this chapter stems. It is located in the southern part of Haiti, approximately two hours' drive from the capital, Port-au-Prince. Jacmel is both nationally and internationally renowned for its natural beauty and long history of cultural and touristic attractions and activities, including art fairs and popular carnivals, which attract people from all over the world. It is surrounded by ocean, mountains, and rivers. Nearly 26,000 people were living there when I visited. Most of them were working-class but there was also a small bourgeoisie. The children of farmers from the impoverished countryside had abandoned their parents' farms and moved to Jacmel in search of a better life. Many had become street vendors or taxi drivers to earn a daily living for themselves and their families.

Field Notes

I draw from field notes to analyze language and class disparities shaping the unequal power relations between affluent Haitians and working-class Haitians in Jacmel,. The field notes that inform this chapter stemmed from daily observations of two distinct classes in Jacmel: the rich, mainly comprising a small group of light-skinned Haitians who controlled the local economy, and the masses, composed largely of poor, working-class, dark-skinned Haitians, who were economically struggling. Interaction between the affluent class and the masses, including their daily use of French (the dominant language) and Creole (the dominant dialect), was documented for analysis.

While living in Jacmel, I looked for ways to be acquainted with the community where I resided. Specifically, I sought opportunities to be immersed in an Afro-centric town called Meyer, located about 15 miles from downtown Jacmel. While living there, I participated in many social and cultural events and social gatherings, both public and private, which enabled me to gain an emic understanding of Meyer. I interacted daily with ordinary working-class farmers and street vendors, as well as the wealthy. I was involved in daily activities that the local people were involved in, like playing dominoes. This allowed me to learn about the history and culture of the community, as I am not originally from there.

Field Notes on Class and Language Disparities

As I gradually became part of the Meyer community, I realized that the bourgeoisie and the masses were segregated by social class, language, and skin color. Differences between the affluent class and the working class lay in taste and style, which seemed fundamentally language- and class-based. Some of the most striking differences lay in the restaurants the affluent class frequented, the brand stores where they purchased the chic clothes they wore for special events, the supermarkets where they bought imported food, the neighborhoods where they lived, the social clubs they were affiliated with, the schools they themselves had attended and to which they sent their children, the foreign languages they had the opportunity to learn and speak fluently, the musical instruments they played, and, finally, the countries they visited for vacation purposes.

The affluent class had businesses in marginalized neighborhoods, as these were economically profitable. They tended to speak multiple languages, including French (the dominant language there), English, and Spanish, and the local language, Creole, which they used to interact with the masses on whom they depended to sell imported products, in order to maximize their profits. Bourdieu (1999, p. 47) notes:

> Imposition of French as the official language did not result in the total abolition of the written use of dialects, whether in administrative, political or even literary texts (dialect literature continued to exist during the *ancien regime*), and their oral uses remained predominant. A situation of bilingualism tended to arise. Whereas the lower classes, particularly the peasantry, were limited to the local dialect, the aristocracy, the commercial and business bourgeoisie and particularly the literate petite bourgeoisie (precisely those who responded to Abbe Gregoire's . . . institutions of linguistic unification) had access much more frequently to the use of the official language . . . (which was still used in most private and even public situations), a situation in which they were destined to fulfill the function of intermediaries.

In Jacmel, linguistic competence in the Creole language was, and continues to be, vitally important for business and political purposes., while French allowed the rich to maintain their social and political status, they used Creole for commercial and business purposes with the masses. The next section further unpacks the unequal power relations between French and Creole while at the same time examining the complex and complicated unequal economic power relations between the rich and the masses living there.

Why Do the Bourgeois Class Need the Poor to Be Rich?

Affluent children attended schools where French was used as the language of instruction, as opposed to poor schools where Creole was the primary language of instruction. Moreover, members of the middle class spoke French exclusively with family members, close friends, and peers, while speaking Creole with the maids who took care of their children. They also used Creole to communicate with local farmers, street vendors, and owners of small businesses, who seemed to depend on them for major purchases of both material products and food.

Language and class privileges determined what kinds of school certain children could afford to attend. For example, the rich schools were sufficiently funded and had well-trained and well-paid teachers. By contrast, poor children attended poorly funded schools, where the language of instruction was Creole and the teachers were poorly trained, overworked, and underpaid. While living in Jacmel, my daughter, who was five years old, attended one of these schools, and she was perceived and treated as a privileged child, which was in fact the case. I wanted her to be at a school where she could experience and bear witness to these class and language disparities.

Besides being favoured by the school system, the affluent class in Jacmel controlled the local economy. Local farmers and street vendors mainly bought food, clothes, and other products in stores owned by the bourgeois class, who also owned supermarkets, gas stations, hotels, and restaurants. Essentially, the bourgeoisie owned the means of production while employing local workers to work for them. Historically, in Haiti, the bourgeois class has monopolized both the local and national economy, and influenced the school system and the political structures of the country (Farmer, 2006).

Many members of the Haitian bourgeoisie are the offspring of former slave masters and enslaved Africans. Fanon (1961, p. 12) observes:

> Spoiled children of yesterday's colonialism and today's governing powers, they oversee the looting of the few national resources. Ruthless in their way scheming and legal pilfering, they use poverty, now nationwide, to work their way to the top through import–export holdings, limited companies, playing the stock market, and nepotism.

In Jacmel, members of the elite class rarely spoke Creole with their children. However, they spoke Creole daily with the maids who worked with them, and the maids spoke Creole with the children. The children essentially learned Creole from the maids, who also served as their nannies. The rich depended on these nannies to watch their children while they socialized with friends at special events, like birthday parties and weddings. They were essentially treated like domestic slaves. For example, on average, they were paid between 50 and 60 dollars a month to clean, cook, iron, and take care of the children daily. Employees often had to work long extra hours in hotels, restaurants, and stores, with no health insurance or paid sick days.

In Jacmel, poor, working-class people were often discriminated against because of their lower-class status, including their inability to speak French, which the bourgeois class mainly used to communicate with one another.

In this context, Creole, is a form of linguistic capital that is needed for commercial and transactional purposes between the bourgeoisie and local consumers. However, once the daily commercial transactions were over, all linguistic and social interaction between the bourgeoisie and the masses ended. Each returned to his/her respective social milieu. In the bourgeois areas, there were relatively paved and clean roads, and electricity was not scarce, in contrast to the marginalized neighborhoods where electricity was scarce. There was also no noise stemming from fights over matters like land disputes and scarcity of food—the bourgeoisie did not argue and kill one another as a result of daily frustration and anger rooted in abject poverty and political corruption.

Furthermore, in the neighborhoods where the bourgeoisie resided, mansions were built by special request and on demand. Supermarkets were accessible with high-quality, healthy food, while the schools had well-prepared and well-supported teachers., these neighborhoods were protected by private security guards and well-trained dogs against potential break-ins by thieves. By contrast, in the neighborhoods where the masses lived, there was constant noise. Loud music was played in night clubs owned by small local businessmen who struggled to keep their enterprises open. There was also a scarcity of electricity, crime was rampant, and there was gambling on every corner where the poor and addicts hung out. There were no health clinics, hospitals, or adequate medical care.

In Jacmel, the bourgeoisie depended on the cheap labour of the masses to sustain their businesses and their families, financially. Without the masses' slave-like labour— the bourgeois class in Jacmel and many other parts of Haiti simply would not survive.

What Does Language Have to Do with Class?

As mentioned, many members of the bourgeois class used Creole to communicate with or give orders to their domestic maids and bodyguards. Many of these servants did not speak French, so their bosses and their children were compelled to speak Creole with them. Language and class disparities were evident in the way the rich treated the poor. The latter comprised struggling working-class farmers, street vendors, and beggars, who were routinely viewed and treated as the scum of the earth—uneducated, loud, and argumentative. These characteristics seemed to be ways of being authentic, at least for the masses; meanwhile, the rich considered them signs of vulgarity. Differences and disparities between these two antagonistic groups were also linked to the social construction of standard French language and Creole. Such a construction appears to serve the interests of those in powerful positions.

In Haiti, French is the dominant language of the middle class and the elite, and it has been imposed on poor, working-class students in schools, even though the majority of Haitians do not speak it (Degraff, 2019; Lefebvre, 2006). Schools play a key role in the construction, reproduction, and legitimation of oppression, including the domination of standard languages and accents through teachers' teaching practices (Livingston et al., 2016; Nelson et al., 2016).

The politics of language hegemony must be understood in order to unpack class disparity in Haiti. During the colonial era, the language of the colonizer group was forcibly imposed upon the colonized as the official and civilized language, while the native tongue of the latter was labelled as "savage". The same form of language hegemony remains prevalent in modern times, although often camouflaged by the dominant discourse of democracy and social justice that is circulated through schools, among other social institutions.

Non-dominant French speakers from working-class backgrounds who live in formerly colonized countries, like Haiti, experience various forms of linguoelitism in schools and society at large. In Haiti, people who speak standard French tend to benefit from greater social mobility and prestige than those who do not, as they are often believed to be more intelligent (Degraff, 2019; Youssef, 2002).

Analysis

As noted earlier, in a putatively post-colonial society like the United States, African American Vernacular English and other minority languages have been constructed as subaltern, and this construction has impacted linguistic minority groups. One's native language should not be labelled subaltern, for such a language reflects one's cultural identity. To label a language subaltern presupposes, for example, that language A (the subordinate language) is inferior to language B (the dominant language). Hence, the sociolinguistic construction of AAVE and other minority languages and accents as subaltern must be rejected in view of the fact that all languages are rule-governed and deeply reflect people's identity and cultural heritage (Baugh, 2010). Likewise, oppressed groups who use their native languages, like Haitian Creole, to affirm their identities should not be discriminated against.

The subaltern label placed on the native tongues of culturally and linguistically diverse groups who have been historically oppressed can be traced back to the colonial era, where privileged and powerful groups and individuals, namely colonizers, imposed their standardized languages and accents on colonized people, whose languages were treated as subaltern. The notion of *standard* has been manufactured, promoted, and sold to the general public for hegemonic linguistic consumption at the expense of minority languages and accents.

People speak multiple languages in different accents. They draw on a variety of linguistic repertoires to communicate their thoughts and emotions. But this creative use of languages in diverse accents is often unappreciated in post-colonial mainstream society. In an evolving multicultural and multilingual world, the standardization and imposition of Western dominant languages and accents on linguistic minorities abroad is insensitive and unjust, as it silences non-dominant languages.

Such unjust linguistic acts have also occurred in the United States, most notably with Ron Unz's fierce campaign to end bilingual education. Unz was, and continues to be, the principal proponent of the "English-only" policies that led to the elimination of bilingual education in many states, including California, Arizona, and Massachusetts (García and Wei, 2014). A large body of research shows that students who are supported in the use of their mother tongue tend to develop stronger cognitive and linguistic abilities as well as higher self-esteem—all of which are conducive to their learning—than those who are not supported in this way (Cummins, 1977; Skutnabb-Kangas, 2000; Valdés, 2005). Hence, discriminating against linguistic minorities because of their dialects and social class poses a danger not only to their inalienable linguistic rights but also to their learning, identities, and material living conditions.

Conclusion

Linguoelitism has no border. It has affected minoritized linguistic groups across the globe. Throughout history, linguistically minoritized groups have been discriminated against because of their native languages and accents, while dominant groups have been granted greater opportunities to maintain their languages and accents at the expense of others. This form of linguistic inequity has affected linguistically and culturally marginalized groups in colonized nations, like Haiti. These groups have been discriminated against because of their native language and accent. This form of linguistic inequity must be accounted for in our analysis and pursuit of linguistic justice (Baugh, 2018).

References

Ahmed, Z. T., Abdullah, A. N., & Heng, C. S. (2013). The Role of Accent and Ethnicity in the Professional and Academic Context. *International Journal of Applied Linguistics and English Literature*, 2(5): 249–258.

Baugh, J. (1999). *Out of the Mouths of Slaves: African American Language and Educational Malpractice*. Austin: University of Texas Press.

Baugh, J. (2010). *Black Street Speech: Its History, Structure, and Survival*. Austin: University of Texas Press.

Baugh, J. (2018). *Linguistics in Pursuit of Justice*. Cambridge: Cambridge University Press.

Bourdieu, P. (1999). *Language and Symbolic Power*. Cambridge, MA: Harvard University Press.

Cummins, J. (1977). Cognitive Factors Associated with the Attainment of Intermediate Levels of Bilingual Skills. *Modern Language Journal*, 61(1–2): 3–12.

Fanon, Frantz. (1961). "The Wretched of the Earth". *Trans. Richard Philcox*. New York: Grove Press 6 (2004).

Farmer, P. (2006). *The Uses of Haiti*. Monroe, ME: Common Courage Press.

García, O., & Wei, L. (2014). Translanguaging and Education. In O. García & L. Wei (Eds.), *Translanguaging: Language, Bilingualism and Education* (pp. 63–77). Basingstoke, UK: Palgrave Macmillan.

Gee, J. (2004). *Situated Language and Learning: A Critique of Traditional Schooling*. London: Routledge.

Gee, J. (2011). *How to Do Discourse Analysis: A Tool Kit*. New York: Routledge.

Gluszek, A., & Dovidio, J. F. (2010). Speaking with a Nonnative Accent: Perceptions of Bias, Communication Difficulties, and Belonging in the United States. *Journal of Language and Social Psychology*, 29(2): 224–234.

Kinzler, K. D., & DeJesus, J. M. (2013). Northern=Smart and Southern=Nice: The Development of Accent Attitudes in the United States. *Quarterly Journal of Experimental Psychology*, 66(6): 1146–1158.

Labov, W. (2011). *Principles of Linguistic Change, Vol. 3: Cognitive and Cultural Factors*. New York: John Wiley & Sons.

Lefebvre, C. (2006). *Creole Genesis and the Acquisition of Grammar: The Case of Haitian Creole*. Cambridge, UK: Cambridge University Press.

Lippi-Green, R. (2012). *English with an Accent: Language, Ideology, and Discrimination in the United States*. New York: Routledge.

Livingston, B. A., Schilpzand, P., & Erez, A. (2016). Not What You Expected to Hear. *Journal of Management*, 43(3): 804–833.

Macedo, D., Dendrinos, B., & Gounari, P. (2015). *Hegemony of English*. New York: Routledge.

Nelson, L. R., Signorella, M. L., & Botti, K. G. (2016). Accent, Gender, and Perceived Competence. *Hispanic Journal of Behavioral Sciences*, 38(2): 166–185.

Neuliep, J. W., & Speten-Hansen, K. M. (2013). The Influence of Ethnocentrism on Social Perceptions of Nonnative Accents. *Language and Communication*, 33(3): 167–176.

Pennycook, A. (2017). *The Cultural Politics of English as an International Language*. New York: Taylor & Francis.

Phillipson, R. (1992). *Linguistic Imperialism*. Oxford, England: Oxford University Press.

Phillipson, R. (2009). *Linguistic Imperialism Continued*. New York: Routledge.

Skutnabb-Kangas, T. (2000). *Linguistic Genocide in Education—or Worldwide Diversity and Human Rights?* New York: Routledge.

Skutnabb-Kangas, T., & Dunbar, R. (2010). *Indigenous Children's Education as Linguistic Genocide and a Crime Against Humanity? A Global View*. Guovdageaidnu: Gáldu.

Smith, A. (2017). *U wot m8? American and British Attitudes Toward Regional British Accents*. Unpublished Senior Thesis. Scripps College. Retrieved on 21/06/2018.

Valdés, G. (2005). Bilingualism, Heritage Language Learners, and SLA Research: Opportunities Lost or Seized? *Modern Language Journal*, 89(3): 410–426.

Youssef, V. (2002). Issues of Bilingual Education in the Caribbean: The Cases of Haiti, and Trinidad and Tobago. *International Journal of Bilingual Education and Bilingualism*, 5(3): 182–193.

Appendix

NARRATIVE

Gender: M
Age: 18
Country of Origin: Philippines
Your social class status (working class, <u>middle class</u>, or upper class)
First Language: Visaya
Name (Pseudonym): N/A
Race/Ethnicity: Filipino

Instruction for Short Narrative

Please describe an accent-based discrimination you might have experienced or you might have witnessed someone (i.e. close friends, family members, co-workers, neighbors, classmates or a stranger) experiencing. Please explain how you felt and continue to feel about this experience. Please be as detailed and specific as possible.

I've seen many people with strong accents or maybe a speech impediment made fun of because of their speech. The most recent experience I can recall is a man being asked being asked for his name [sic] in the first day of class with either an accent or a speech impediment. It was very hard to understand his name, but it turns out it was "Ralph". He was made fun of and laughed at by the other kids in class.

Have you or do you know anyone who might have been discriminated against because of his/her accent? If so, please would you describe how and where?

Made a note: "On the front page"

Do you believe that people who speak with an accent or certain types of accents may be less smart than those who do not? Please explain in detail.

No, because I know a lot of smart immigrants with accents.

NARRATIVE

Gender: M
Date: 6/18/14
Age: 24
Country of Origin: Pakistan
Your social class status (working class, middle class, or upper class)
First Language: Pashto
Name (pseudonym): Fahd
Nationality: USA
Race/Ethnicity: Palthan (Asian)

Instruction for Short Narrative

Please describe an accent-based discrimination you might have experienced or you might have witnessed someone (i.e. close friends, family members, co-workers, neighbors, classmates or a stranger) experienced. Please explain how you felt and continue to feel about this experience. Please be as detailed and specific as possible.

N/A

Have you or do you know anyone who might have been discriminated against because of his/her accent? If so, please would you describe how and where?

No.

Do you believe that people who speak with an accent or certain types of accents may be less smart than those who do not? Please explain in detail.

No, I do not believe that people who speak with an accent or certain types of accents may be less smart than those who do not because the smartness of a person is not based on their accent. Accent has nothing to do with the smartness.

NARRATIVE

Gender: F
Date: 3/16/14
Age: 18
Country of Origin: N/A
Your social class status (working class, <u>middle class</u>, or upper class)
First Language: Gujarati
Name (Pseudonym): N/A
Nationality: N/A
Race/Ethnicity: Asian

Instruction for Short Narrative

Please describe an accent-based discrimination you might have experienced or you might have witnessed someone (i.e. close friends, family members, co-workers, neighbors, classmates or a stranger) experienced. Please explain how you felt and continue to feel about this experience. Please be as detailed and specific as possible.

There was this new student in my class a few years ago, and he had just immigrated to USA, therefore he still had a thick accent. However, it came time to work in groups, no one would ever pair up with him and whenever he talked people would laugh. I would sometimes pair up with him if I didn't have a partner. I always felt bad and will continue to feel bad.

Have you or do you know anyone who might have been discriminated against because of his/her accent? If so, please would you describe how and where?

N/A

Do you believe that people who speak with an accent or certain types of accents may be less smart than those who do not? Please explain in detail.

No, because it all depends on the quality of education you receive and how well you take advantage of it.

NARRATIVE

Gender: M
Date: 6/18/14
Age: 26
Country of Origin: United States
Your social class status (working class, <u>middle class</u>, or upper class)
First Language: English
Name (Pseudonym): Chris Frey
Nationality: American
Race/Ethnicity: Caucasian

Instruction for Short Narrative

Please describe an accent-based discrimination you might have experienced or you might have witnessed someone (i.e. close friends, family members, co-workers, neighbors, classmates or a stranger) experienced. Please explain how you felt and continue to feel about this experience. Please be as detailed and specific as possible.

N/A

Have you or do you know anyone who might have been discriminated against because of his/her accent? If so, please would you describe how and where?

I do not know anyone who has been discriminated against because his or her accent.

Do you believe that people who speak with an accent or certain types of accents may be less smart than those who do not? Please explain in detail.

I believe those who speak with an accent or certain types of accents are equally smart as those <u>with not certain accent</u>. The way he sound when we speak does not necessarily reflect how intelligent we are.

NARRATIVE

Gender: M
Date: 4/15/14
Age: 19
Your social class status (<u>working class</u>, middle class, or upper class)
First Language: Gujarati
Name (Pseudonym): N/A
Nationality: Indian
Race/Ethnicity: Indian [Asian]

Instruction for Short Narrative

Please describe an accent-based discrimination you might have experienced or you might have witnessed someone (i.e. close friends, family members, co-workers, neighbors, classmates or a stranger) experienced. Please explain how you felt and continue to feel about this experience. Please be as detailed and specific as possible.

There was this new student in my class a few years ago, and he had just immigrated to U.S.A., therefore he still had a thick accent. However, it came time to work in groups, no one would ever pair up with him and whenever he talked people would laugh. I would sometimes pair up with if I didn't have a partner. I always felt bad and will continue to feel bad.

Have you or do you know anyone who might have been discriminated against because of his/her accent? If so, please would you describe how and where?

[sic] Answer→ I came to U.S.A. as a junior in high xchool at age of 17. In high xchool I did notice a guy with a thick [Indian] accent. He was a nice person, really polite and respectful, but the only reason he had hard time making friends was because of his accent. The discrimination I noticed was social discrimination. Despite of him being nice, people avoided him, called him names like "FOB". I remember helping him in Math and English in ESL (English as a Second Language). He was a great guy, he noticed social discrimination and just smiled at how people reacted.

Do you believe that people who speak with an accent or certain types of accents may be less smart than those who do not? Please explain in detail.

Answer→ According to me, accent cannot be used as a factor to judge someone's smartness. I have a cousin who has good grammar skills, but has an accent. He is a Senior Software Developer in multinational company. I have [a] better accent than him, but I still look up to him as inspiration because I am a computer science major. Another example would be our [Calculus] professor. Astu-Swanzy, he is one of the smartest [teachers] I have had in my life. Despite his thick accent, I understand everything in his class.

NARRATIVE

Gender: M
Date: 6/31/14
Age: 18
Your social class status (<u>working class</u>, middle class, or upper class)
First Language: Spanish
Name (Pseudonym): Kelvin G.
Country of Origin: Puerto Rico
Race/Ethnicity: N/A

Instruction for Short Narrative

Please describe an accent-based discrimination you might have experienced or you might have witnessed someone (i.e. close friends, family members, co-workers, neighbors, classmates or a stranger) experienced. Please explain how you felt and continue to feel about this experience. Please be as detailed and specific as possible.

When I was about ten years old, the kids in my classroom used to make fun of my accent. At first, I did not know why they were laughing, but then I know. I got used to it after a while and in the meantime I worked really hard to learn English fast, and I did.

Have you or do you know anyone who might have been discriminated against because of his/her accent? If so, please would you describe how and where?

N/A

> Do you believe that people who speak with an accent or certain types of accents may be less smart than those who do not? Please explain in detail.

No, I do not. I believe someone with an accent is just as capable as anyone else.

NARRATIVE

Gender: M
Date: 4/17/14
Age: 27
Your social class status (<u>working class</u>**, middle class, or upper class)**
First Language: Spanish
Name (Pseudonym): Leo
Country of Origin: Ecuador
Race/Ethnicity: Hispanic

Instruction for Short Narrative

> Please describe an accent-based discrimination you might have experienced or you might have witnessed someone (i.e. close friends, family members, co-workers, neighbors, classmates or a stranger) experienced. Please explain how you felt and continue to feel about this experience. Please be as detailed and specific as possible.

Well, I have experienced laughs from other people, friends, coworkers and it makes me feel uncomfortable, but not discriminated [against]. I think when people make fun of other [foreign] people it's kind of rude. The only time I felt discriminated [against] is when other people don't take me as serious just because of my accent.

> Have you or do you know anyone who might have been discriminated against because of his/her accent? If so, please would you describe how and where?

I have [worked] in many casinos and I have [witnessed] people being mistreated for not speaking [sic] fluidly English.

> Do you believe that people who speak with an accent or certain types of accents may be less smart than those who do not? Please explain in detail.

No, I do not believe such [a] thing. Accent has nothing to do with being smart.

NARRATIVE

Gender: F
Date: 7/1/14
Age: 20
Your social class status (<u>working class</u>, <u>middle class</u>, or upper class)
First Language: English
Name (Pseudonym): Shan
Country of Origin: USA
Race/Ethnicity: White

Instruction for Short Narrative

Please describe an accent-based discrimination you might have experienced or you might have witnessed someone (i.e. close friends, family members, co-workers, neighbors, classmates or a stranger) experienced. Please explain how you felt and continue to feel about this experience. Please be as detailed and specific as possible.

A few years back I witnessed one of my co-workers/friends get yelled at and called names at my workplace because a rude customer didn't receive the right size of what they ordered.

Have you or do you know anyone who might have been discriminated against because of his/her accent? If so, please would you describe how and where?

Yes, I have witnessed a few accounts of discrimination between many people in my workplace and friends. It all starts with people with a bad mood/temper and one little thing will set it off and then people say what they don't mean, and people become hurt.

Do you believe that people who speak with an accent or certain types of accents may be less smart than those who do not? Please explain in detail.

No, people with accents are just as smart as people without accents. They might struggle some because it is a new [sic] language and text to them, but that doesn't make them stupid/smart.

NARRATIVE

Gender: M
Date: 4/11/14
Age: 23
Your social class status (<u>working class</u>, middle class, or upper class)
First Language: Twi
Name (Pseudonym): Jak
Country of Origin: Ghana
Race/Ethnicity: Not Hispanic or Latino

Instruction for Short Narrative

Please describe an accent-based discrimination you might have experienced or you might have witnessed someone (i.e. close friends, family members, co-workers, neighbors, classmates or a stranger) experienced. Please explain how you felt and continue to feel about this experience. Please be as detailed and specific as possible.

When I first started college, I had been at [sic] the state for a couple of months, so my accent was very [sic] huge. Any time I tried to ask [a] question in class, I could see some of the students giggling. It continued for a while which made me [feel] embarrassed and never wanted to speak, utter a word again in class, but the class instructor stepped in and [warned] those students, [sic] rather than that I was always overwhelmed with fear when lessons [were] due. **Have you or do you know anyone who might have been discriminated against because of his/her accent? If so, please would you describe how and where?**

N/A

Do you believe that people who speak with an accent or certain types of accents may be less smart than those who do not? Please explain in detail.

Having an accent doesn't make you dumb or less smart. It is just a [sic] tongue different. If anyone tries to learn a new language, he/she can't speak it clearly as a native from that land. It is obvious. From my observation, having an accent doesn't make you unclever. [I] am a student from ACCC and I could tell that especially foreign students over there are very smart when it comes to STEM programs. These kinds of programs [have] nothing to do with fluency, and, from my observations, foreigners who [have] been stereotyped as having accents excel better than the natives. Smartness does not depend on accent, but your IQ and EQ.

NARRATIVE

Gender: M
Date: 4/15/14
Age: 23
Your social class status (working class, middle class, or upper class) N/A
First Language: Igbo
Name (Pseudonym): Ibex
Country of Origin: Nigeria
Race/Ethnicity: Black/African-American
Your status (student, teacher, mother, father, etc.)

Instruction for Short Narrative

Please describe an accent-based discrimination you might have experienced or you might have witnessed someone (i.e. close friends, family members, co-workers, neighbors, classmates or a stranger) experienced. Please explain how you felt and continue to feel about this experience. Please be as detailed and specific as possible.

I have experienced a discrimination at work. There is this co-worker who [has] a heavy accent and went to the H.R. to complain, but his case was dismissed because he could not speak clearly.

Have you or do you know anyone who might have been discriminated against because of his/her accent? If so, please would you describe how and where?

I have experienced [discrimination] in class; this happens when I try to answer a question. I tried to express my answer, but the teacher claims that she can't understand me. Moreover, I was in my clear in my explanation.

Do you believe that people who speak with an accent or certain types of accents may be less smart than those who do not? Please explain in detail.
Yes, I do not believe that people who speak with [an] accent may be less smart than those who do not. This is because students with accents are smarter, but the problem they are facing is to express their knowledge, because, when they speak, the teacher or student may not understand.

NARRATIVE

Gender: F
Date: 7/1/14
Age: 19
Your social class status (working class, <u>middle class</u>, or upper class)
First Language: English
Name (Pseudonym): Kellsy
Country of Origin: USA
Nationality: German
Race/Ethnicity: White

Instruction for Short Narrative

Please describe an accent-based discrimination you might have experienced or you might have witnessed someone (i.e. close friends, family members, co-workers, neighbors, classmates or a stranger) experienced. Please explain how you felt and continue to feel about this experience. Please be as detailed and specific as possible.
I have a friend from England at school with a British accent and people laugh when she talks and usually don't take her [seriously]. It makes me feel bad because it is something she can't control.

Have you or do you know anyone who might have been discriminated against because of his/her accent? If so, please would you describe how and where?
Yes, people laugh when she talks, and they don't take her [seriously]. She is from England.

> Do you believe that people who speak with an accent or certain types of accents may be less smart than those who do not? Please explain in detail.
> No, I don't think so at all. I know people with accents who are very intelligent.

NARRATIVE

Gender: F
Date: 7/1/14
Age: 21
Your social class status (<u>working class</u>, middle class, or upper class)
First Language: Haitian Creole
Name (Pseudonym): N/A
Country of Origin: Haiti
Race/Ethnicity: "Black Haitian"

Instruction for Short Narrative

> Please describe an accent-based discrimination you might have experienced or you might have witnessed someone (i.e. close friends, family members, co-workers, neighbors, classmates or a stranger) experienced. Please explain how you felt and continue to feel about this experience. Please be as detailed and specific as possible.

People who discriminated other people because their accent are dumb. They are not smart enough to understand those people can speak more than [one] language.

> Have you or do you know anyone who might have been discriminated against because of his/her accent? If so, please would you describe how and where?

No.

> Do you believe that people who speak with an accent or certain types of accents may be less smart than those who do not? Please explain in detail.

No, in contrary people who speak with an accent [are] fortunate to speak another language. If somebody was not born in a country and can speak that country's language, it does not matter if you have [an] accent or not that person is special.

NARRATIVE

Gender: F
Date: 7/1/14
Age: 24
Your social class status (<u>working class</u>, middle class, or upper class)
First Language: English
Name (Pseudonym): Aseya
Country of Origin: USA
Race/Ethnicity: Black/African-American

Instruction for Short Narrative

Please describe an accent-based discrimination you might have experienced or you might have witnessed someone (i.e. close friends, family members, co-workers, neighbors, classmates or a stranger) experienced. Please explain how you felt and continue to feel about this experience. Please be as detailed and specific as possible.

When I was younger, my mother had an Egyptian friend that was having a hard time adjusting to living in America. My mother would make me go to the supermarket and other stores with her to help out. I can recall how people would treat me, a nine-year-old, with more respect and kindness than they did Ms. Hannah, because I spoke English and she had an accent.

Have you or do you know anyone who might have been discriminated against because of his/her accent? If so, please would you describe how and where?

My mother's friend would get treated like a low-class citizen because of her Egyptian accent. People would get frustrated because they couldn't understand her and yell curses and tell her to go back to her country.

Do you believe that people who speak with an accent or certain types of accents may be less smart than those who do not? Please explain in detail.

I do not believe people that speak with accents [are less] smart. In reality, everyone speaks with an accent of some sort. The way a person speaks [does] not, [sic] or is not, determined or correlated with how they think or perceive things. An accent comes from the region you live in and even if you didn't grow up in a place if you live there long enough you will pick up that accent. Education and intelligence come from the cognition of the brain. The two have no effect on each other.

Mari

Linguicism, or racism expressed through the vehicle of language, has many manifestations. Among these are English-only policies, accent discrimination, and prejudice based on word choice. I have most directly experienced linguicism via my accent and choice of words. As a Chicana in a society which seldom views Mexican Americans as authority figures on language and/or communication, I have experienced a trend of being "questioned", "corrected", and "helped" with my pronunciation and choice of words. I studied communication and accents in graduate school. I am informed and aware that every person speaks with an accent. I know that to what people are usually referring when they comment that another speaks "with an accent" is the regionalism that distinguishes "the sound" of one group of people from another. I know that accent is about inflection and about pattern of pitch, but also often about word choice.

I remember vividly being in seventh grade and explaining to a teacher that the description provided in our book seemed "stereotypical" to me. The teacher, a White woman working in a predominantly Chicano community, stopped me to correct that the word "stereotypical" did not exist and that I should choose other language to describe my point. I respected this teacher and her authority, so I did not respond. I was left with doubt, feeling certain that the word existed, but believing that if this teacher advised me otherwise, I must indeed be wrong. Perhaps my act of resistance was in going home to search for myself. I consulted a Webster's Dictionary and found that the word exists. Of course, what then ensued was bewilderment. Why had I been corrected? Did my teacher not know about this word? Another memorable example of linguicism happened to me when I was working as a professional, right out of college. I remember describing to my boss (White male with a Ph.D.) that I had been raised in a mountainous region of the country. Almost 15 years later, I can still see the smug expression on his face as he interrupted my description of home to inform me that "mountainous" was not a word. By then, I had experienced plenty of racism, and specifically linguicism. So I responded that I was pretty certain the word existed. His comment then to me was that his Ph.D. was in English language and that he would leave it at that. I'm not sure what I find more problematic as I think back about this now: that this person had a Ph.D. in English language and did not know the word mountainous, or that I retreated to my office to look up the word as I was once again seeped in doubt. The most common example of linguicism as it pertains to the sound of my particular accent is that I often surprise people for sounding as I do in either English or Spanish. I have been told time and again that it's surprising I speak my English without a "Mexican" accent and that I pronounce words "so well" as if pronouncing them with a different accent would interrupt their wellness. In true form to my Chicana experience, living in the liminal space of neither here nor there, I have similarly been told by Spanish speakers that it is unfathomable that I speak Spanish so properly and without sounding like a "gringa". In people's assessment of my use of either language, I am positioned as different/other/anomaly. Otherwise, why point it out? Is it my sound or their hearing that is actually to be pointed out? I have been "instructed/corrected/enlightened" about the words I choose to express myself and the way in which I sound at many times in my life, both personally and professionally. What is problematic about incidents of linguicism is that they are not simply "corrections", made from one person to another. Rather, acts of linguicism are acts of denigration and subjugation. The relationships between a teacher and student, a boss and employee, etc. are based on power. The act of "correcting" is an act of pointing a finger, cornering, marginalizing, and putting someone in her place. It is an interruption to the storytelling, an attempt to manipulate the narration, and a hyper act of situating someone away from the center, even of her own story.

As a former secondary education English teacher, Donna has worked in urban communities for nearly a decade; she currently works as a consultant with the State College Area School District in their Professional Development School.

I was born and raised in Jamaica, and it hadn't occurred to me when I left Jamaica for the U.S. that my dialect would somehow come to define so much of my social and academic identities. Almost immediately, as I arrived my teacher wanted to place me in a bilingual class, never mind that I spoke English. My accent was enough to distinguish me as a non-standard English speaker (my teacher thought I was speaking French Creole). It seemed immediately that I had to abandon my patois dialect, and adopt a more standardized variety of English. My brother and I practiced our "American" daily. We dropped "Mummy" for "Mom", and adopted "Ain't" and "Y'all", as new markers for our identity as Americans. For a long time this worked, or maybe it was just that we didn't stand out amongst the other Caribbean immigrants in New York. However, after leaving the public schools of NYC for college/higher ed made me realize that my speech mattered more than ever, and the more I spoke the more I realized that how I spoke—simple utterances—revealed more about me than I possibly could, and so writing became my refuge. It was the one place where I could be inconspicuous, and unburdened by my accent, my speech, and by my inability to perform standard English in the ways that society finds acceptable.

Consequently, my language, speech, and accent are always in flux. One moment my students are asking me to repeat myself because they're not sure about a word I just said; in another instance my daughter points out that there is something peculiar about the way that I say certain words (this has done a lot to entertain her six-year-old mind). While at other times my family and friends in Jamaica tell me they are unclear about what I have said or the meaning I am aiming to convey. The complexity of my language experience has made me realize that I sort of exist in an imperfect speech place. I can no longer master my first dialect, and yet I am still not able to master the standard variety I engage with daily. I am self-conscious often especially because, unlike my friends who do speak other languages, English is my first language. What then is my excuse for not being able to follow the rules of standard English speech? I would like to end by telling you that I have reached a place where I am comfortable, where I feel content in my abilities as a speaker of English, but I cannot. I still struggle daily to follow those simple rules in my speech that comes so easy for me with the written text. I sometimes find myself writing down my response to something, just so I can have it right and ready for verbal articulation. I am not sure that I will ever reach a place where my speech will be clearly understood by everyone, and I am not certain that's as important to me today as it once was.

Deba

It's a beautiful April evening canopied with a shimmering cerulean sky that you only see here in our sun-bathed city, Las Cruces, New Mexico. Facing the Aggie Mountain, the Farm and Ranch Heritage Museum sits close to it while the desert landscape skirts it from all the other sides. An audience eagerly waits for the Indian dancer in the cozy auditorium nestled inside the museum. She will soon be performing Bharatanatyam, an ancient classical genre of dance that takes years of training for the dancer to perfect.

It is going to be a treat! In Kolkata, India, I often attended dance recitals, and some of my friends and family members were well-trained dancers. But how many times have I experienced something like this in Las Cruces since my arrival here in 1993, in this long thirteen years? Well, never so far! A happy excitement stirring inside makes me giddy! I look around; the hall is nearly full. The hum falling and rising from all the talking is comforting. A lady is there sitting by me. She and I, too, begin chit-chatting about this and that. Where are you from? Kolkata, India. Oh how I love talking about my country and my hustling and bustling city! What brings you here? Well, my husband's work. The questioning continues: What do you do? I tell her I teach English at the community college here in town. She pauses, stares at me, and breaks into a laugh. I don't hear the hum anymore. Suddenly, the world around me falls silent while her laugh in my head keeps on ringing and ringing.

Sometimes students who do not do well in my composition course leave comments in the course evaluation that they do not understand the content because of my accent (these comments, however, are few and far between).

Negrette

When I think about any experiences with accent discrimination throughout my personal and professional journey, many incidents come to mind. As an ESL teacher overseas, it was very common to hear people always commenting on my "non-native" accent. In China, for example, my American boss had to work really hard to convince his Chinese wife that my "accent" was not too bad. She was worried that my appearance (dark complexion) along with my accent did not embody the "ideal" English teacher (White, American/British, blonde hair, and blue/green eyes) for the school.

The following are three particular incidents that I remember from my professional and personal journey:

1. As the coordinator of a children's program, I was in charge of overseeing groups of young volunteers from different states in the U.S. These undergraduate students spent their summer helping with our summer ESL camps. I specifically remember one of the volunteers telling me how "thick" my accent was in English and how difficult it was for him to understand me. From that incident, I particularly remember the emphatic way in which this male White American student made me feel that, no matter how qualified and professionally capable I was as an ESL teacher, my English language skills were not good enough, because I didn't have a "native" accent.
2. A person from Australia invited me to have dinner at her place. In this occasion, I went there with my boyfriend, who is American. The next time this person from Australia met my boyfriend, she asked him if we had communication issues in our relationship. She told him, "It must be very difficult for you to be in a relationship with someone who is not a native English speaker. Her accent is very strong". She was laughing about it. As you can imagine, when my boyfriend told me, I did not find it funny at all. On the contrary, situations like that affected my personal and professional confidence.
3. The third incident is connected to the second one. As a "native" English speaker, my boyfriend had mentioned numerous times to me that in order to be taken seriously as a professional in this country, I had to do something about my accent. He reminded me about the incident with the Australian lady and recommended me to sign up for accent reduction therapy. So, for two years I went to the Speech and hearing

clinic to work on accent reduction. I'm not sure if the therapy helped to "reduce" my accent, but what I can say for sure is that I was always very aware of it, and I did not like to speak in front of groups of people, because I was always very self-conscious about my accent.

Participants' Perceptions of, Position about, and Attitude Toward Accent

Maria's *testimonio*: My story is a little different. My father learned Spanish first (seeing that he was born in Mexico) and later in life learned English (just before I was born). My mother (born in the United States) learned English and then Spanish. When I was born, my mother thought it was important for me to learn English (schooling purposes) and then Spanish, shortly after starting kindergarten. I never had an accent, at least not one that was noticeable. So, going to school was never difficult in terms of language. One thing I did notice as I grew up was that my father did have an accent. I was embarrassed of my father, growing up. I didn't want him talking to my friends, nor did I want him attending school functions, because the way in which he would pronounce words.

Elva's *testimonio*: I have always been the type of person who admire accent since I was little. I never thought of accent being a bad thing or making a person less. I always wanted or wished I, myself, had an accent. My sister and I always had fun trying to talk in different accents because we thought it was cool to sound like someone who wasn't from the local area

Jose's *testimonio*: Spanish is my first language, but I learned English when I was very young so I have learned it and use it constantly. But even though I learned it at a young age, I believe I have an accent. This had taken control of my life for a long time, but now I feel more relaxed and not ashamed of my accent. I have more confidence speaking out loud in class or with a big group of people. Thank God I have never been made fun of because of my accent, but now what I realize is that I was holding myself back and judging myself hard. School has helped me understand that our differences are beautiful and how everything makes us who we are. My parents have recently learned how to speak English, and, even though they do have an accent, they are proud of it, because they would never hide who they are and where they came from.

Josefina's *testimonio*: My experience with accent is that myself as a Hispanic I have an accent. I had never really noticed it until my brother told me. When he tells me I have an accent, it doesn't bother me; I just tell him we are all different. I have been around people who speak Spanish, and they have a heavy accent, and I can notice it right away. Mostly those people were born in Mexico, and they have a really different accent. For me, it doesn't bother me, because everyone is unique. My friends also have an accent like me, and I can't even notice it, because I am already used to it. For me, accents show that we are different and shouldn't be judge for it.

Huerta's *testimonio*: When I began attending school, I had teachers who spoke with an accent. At first it was hard to understand the teacher, but after a few weeks I was able to understand him/her. I remember having a math teacher who had a heavy accent; when I first enter his class, I thought to myself, how am I going to understand what he is teaching me? I can honestly say I learned so much more from him about math than I had in all my previous years. He was able to help me better understand now the material. I would say I misjudged him and thought I wasn't going to be able to understand him, but I was able to; now I don't have the same perception I did before having him as a professor. When I began working at Macys, I was amazed to hear so many accents. It was more astonishing to have someone tell me I have an accent. I never thought I did until a couple told me the way I spoke Spanish was very different, not just by now I pronounce words but the fact I had an accent. When you are surrounded by people who speak like you then have someone from out of the town say you have an accent was surprising. I hardly ever hear people tell me that.

Participants' Experiences with Accent Discrimination

Monica's *testimonio:* I recall my first awkward experience from when I was in London at a train station. I was conversing with my sister about the beautiful architecture, with no accents, just our "normal" English accent, and this guy, apparently a little drunk, as he was being supported by two friends, walks by and he asks me, "Are you American?" (In his Brit accent), so a little embarrassed, I answered, "Yes", a little confused. But then he says, "I f*ckin knew it!" Then him and his friend walked away laughing. I was sure how I felt, I was a proud American, but the way I talked made me feel a little embarrassed, because it made me stick out and obvious to other people I was probably just another American tourist. My sister and I kind of laugh and still reenact that scene from time to time with each other to have a laugh, but at that moment, it wasn't as funny. I'm just glad my family was there to help make my awkwardness fade away.

Freda's *testimonio*: I have been told time and again that it's surprising I speak my English without a "Mexican" accent and that I pronounce words "so well", as if pronouncing them with a different accent would interrupt their wellness. In true form to my Chicana experience, living in the liminal space of neither here nor there, I have similarly been told by Spanish speakers that it is unfathomable that I speak Spanish so properly and without sounding like a "gringa". In people's assessment of my use of either language, I am positioned as different/other/anomaly. Otherwise, why point it out? Is it my sound or their hearing that is actually to be pointed out?

Jennifer's *testimonio*: All my life, I have hated my voice. I am from New Orleans, LA, and I am reminded often that I do not sound like I am from New Orleans. I guess that could be a compliment, but I am never sure. When I lived in the Northeast, the students told me that they could not tell that I was from the South. However, my husband's Southern accent is more pronounced than mine, and he received negative feedback regularly.

My challenge came once when I wore a decorative head wrap to a car dealership. One of my students had visited Greece and bought me a wrap. I was launching a complaint in the car dealership, and I thought I was very clear about my complaint. I thought I had been charged for a diagnostic that was attributed to a recalled part. I thought I should not have to pay the diagnostic fee, so I requested a refund. The White woman became very angry and called over a Hispanic guy to "deal with me" because I wasn't speaking English. I was disturbed by that because the only thing I think she did was look at the ethnic head wrap and made assumptions about my ethnicity. I explained to the gentleman that I was not sure which language she thought I was speaking, but I assured him that English was my primary language.

Manoucheca's *testimonio*: My experiences with accent as an educated woman who came from Southeast Asia and lived in the United States for 27 years have been challenging. My most recent experience was at Walmart counter where a cashier, upon seeing me and hearing my accent, started the conversation about, "I am so impressed that your country really perfected making freeze dried food". I said, "Did you mean Japan?" She said, "yes". I replied, "But I'm not Japanese". She said, "You know what I mean".

Chiquita's *testimonio*: When I think about any experiences with accent discrimination throughout my personal and professional journey, many incidents come to mind. As an ESL teacher overseas, it was very common to hear people always commenting on my "non-native" accent. In China, for example, my American boss had to work really hard to convince his Chinese wife that my "accent" was not too bad. She was worried that my appearance (dark complexion) along with my accent did not embody the "ideal" English teacher (White, American/British, blonde hair, and blue/green eyes) for the school.

Santa's *testimonio*: A lady is there sitting by me. She and I, too, begin chit-chatting about this and that. Where are you from? Kolkata, India. Oh how I love talking about my country and my hustling and bustling city! What brings you here? Well, my husband's work. The questioning continues: What do you do? I tell her I teach English at the community college here in town. She pauses, stares at me, and breaks into a laugh. I don't hear the hum anymore. Suddenly, the world around me falls silent while her laugh in my head keeps on ringing and ringing.

James's *testimonio*: I was born and raised in Jamaica, and it hadn't occurred to me when I left Jamaica for the US that my dialect would somehow come to define so much of my social and academic identities. Almost immediately as I arrived, my teacher wanted to place me in a bilingual class, never mind that I spoke English. My accent was enough to distinguish me as a non-standard English speaker (my teacher thought I was speaking French Creole).

Andres' *testimonio*: Accent discrimination in my professional life has come in several ways. It was widespread among fellow graduate students when I first arrived to the U.S. and started an M.A. program in history at Temple University. Some of my classmates just didn't have the patience to listen to me, and zoned out every time I presented or commented in class during my first year in that program. It took me a while to get the handle of it, and I used to get incredibly embarrassed by it, to the point that I spoke as little as possible in class. But I worked on my "accent" and practiced words that were hard to pronounce before going to class. At the University of Massachusetts the discrimination came from a professor who not only wrote in my first evaluation that my accent in English made me difficult to understand, but who also rejected my Spanish because she was used to "Colombian and Mexican Spanish which were superior to Caribbean Spanish".

Melinda's *testimonio*: Because of my distinct accent, I have experienced multiple situations in which it was perceived and commented on. One of the experiences I remember the most was when I was introduced to a lady who commented that my accent was very cute. She seemed really interested in knowing more about me: my nationality, my job, etc. By her comment, I think she really thought she was complimenting me and the way I speak. However, she made me feel that I was different to her and the rest of "natives". Me sounding "cute" was a form of discrimination that I did not like or appreciate. I was discriminated against with what she said, what can be called positive discrimination, still discrimination.

Baltazar's *testimonio*: When some people have asked me where I'm from, and when I say Spain, some of them seem to kind of celebrate. However, when they ask my wife, who is from Ecuador, I notice they don't celebrate anything. Although some people probably celebrate because they know more about Spain than about Ecuador, it seems that some people seem to celebrate more some countries over others, same as they do with races. They probably celebrate some countries over others influenced by country variables, such as race (people in Spain are lighter than in Ecuador, a country that is more associated to Indigenous peoples), ethnicity (the culture in Spain is better considered than the culture in Ecuador), class (a European country versus a third-world country), and language (some people tell me about the Castilian Spanish and insist that the Spanish from Spain is the correct and formal Spanish and that Spanish in Latin America is wrong, informal, and non-educated). This represents accent discrimination and shows deficit discourses trying to privilege a non-standard accent over another type non-standard accent. In this case, those discourses are oppressive to non-standard accents associated to Mexicans and other Spanish-speaking countries.

Naomi's *Testimonio*: Discrimination/ignoring or complaining because of my Spanish accent in English is a regular experience, although it has become less frequent, I guess because I have developed a less "heavy" accent. For instance, at stores I have been ignored, or they have offered to call a person who "speaks Spanish" to "help" me. As I speak, students or other people noticeably go deaf or complain that they do not understand me because of my "accent". After 15+ years teaching at the university level in the US, I have developed strategies to augment my speaking with ways to visualize or read in addition to listening to what I say. There are still students who complain in code about my accent. The latest anonymous comment to the question, "How can this course be improved?" "Having an instructor I can understand when they [sic] are talking".

Participants' Contradiction Statements

Juan's *testimonio*: I have really not experienced discrimination because of my accent, but I have had experience in which they correct or laugh at the way I say things. Such as when I say the "ch" sound in "chair" people make fun of me and say "<u>ch</u>air" or "share". This has made me more aware and makes me somewhat nervous when I speak, because I don't want to say the wrong format of a word. Also, when I travel to Mexico, my cousins make fun of the way I speak because they say it is not proper. So, either way, wherever I go, people continue to pick those things of my language. I could see why it would be difficult for someone to be discriminated because of their accent. Accents are not all accepted, and some people see it as a bad thing and may ridicule them because of the way certain sounds are made. For me, this would make me feel ashamed of my accent, and it would somewhat encourage me to constantly correct the way I am saying things.

Jessica's *testimonio*: I would love to help you, but I really don't feel like I have been discriminated against because of my accent. Most people who pick up on it often think it's cool that I am from Jamaica. If nothing else, it often turns into a conversation about Jamaica and my journey to where I currently am.

I am originally from Eritrea, a country in the Horn of Africa. I came to the U.S. on a government scholarship for a master's degree in my field. That was in 1969. Although I completed my undergraduate studies in English, since English was used at the University in Ethiopia (Eritrea was under Ethiopia at that time), and had taught as an adjunct instructor at the University of Ethiopia, I was shocked when people in the U.S. could not understand me due to my heavy Ethiopian/Eritrean accent. It was very frustrating when I had to repeat myself several times to be understood. I was an excellent student, and my accent did not cause me much of a problem, although I was feeling the pain when I see my professors having a hard time understand me. But I have never experienced being discriminated against because of my accent. However, I suspect that I have missed some promotion opportunities due to my accent. In class, I have some students who comment on the course evaluation saying, "He is teaching a tough course and he is making the course more difficult by his accent". But such comments were from few students. Despite my accent, I have won several teaching excellence awards over the years.

CONSENT FORM

February 20, 2015
Pierre W. Orelus
Principal investigator

Consent Form Project Title and Subtitle: Accent Equality: Against Accentism in Schools and Society.

Dear . . . ,

You are cordially invited to participate in an empirical study on accent that I am conducting. This study examines accent-based discrimination and the emotional, educational, and socio- economic effects this form of discrimination might have had on people, particularly linguistically and culturally diverse groups speaking English with a non-dominant accent. To this end, I am planning on inviting approximately 100 subjects speaking English with a distinct accent to participate in this study. I am seeking from participants insights on accents and accent-based discrimination.

To my knowledge, there are not many studies that have addressed issues related to accent, particularly accent-based discrimination. Therefore, this study will be among the few studies that have explored this issue. I anticipate findings from the study will provide critical insights about people's perception on accents and the manner in which people, including professionals, have been discriminated against because of their non-mainstream accents, and the degree to which this form of discrimination might have affected their personal, psychological, socio-economic, educational, and professional lives.

Your participation in this research is invaluable. However, you are not obligated to participate in it, and your can redraw from it anytime without prejudice. The information you provide will be used during this study for research purposes. I anticipate using data collected for this study to present scholarly papers at conferences and publish research articles in peer reviewed journals. I will also use the data to write a book on accent a year or two after completion of study. Your real name will not be used anywhere in any document, written or otherwise. Instead, a pseudonym will be used to protect your identity.

I appreciate your consideration to this invitation.
Sincerely,
Pierre W. Orelus

Please print your full name, date, and sign below if you agree with the terms of this consent form.

Printed Name___ _____

Signature _____

Index

Abdel (pseudonym) 46–47, 51
Aboriginal children 5
accent discrimination: causes and effects of 44–48, 69; linguistic minorities experiencing 44–48, 51–52; narratives 85–102; participants' testimonios about immigrants facing 48–50; participants whose first language is English 26–31; participants whose first language is Spanish 31–36; standard accent hegemony 15–19; subaltern professors/students 52–56, 58–66, 98–102
accent diversity 37–38, 69, 71–72
accent equity 69, 71–72
accent identity 23–24
accent inclusion 37–38, 69, 71–72
accent inequity 17
accentism 41–42, 51
African Americans 18, 24, 28–30, 35, 36, 40, 41, 46, 48, 51, 64, 70, 71, 75–76, 81
African American Vernacular English (AAVE) 30–31, 72, 70, 81
African children 5–6
African people 17, 51
Akayla (pseudonym) 49–50
American English accents 16–18, 23, 24–25, 27, 29–30, 34–35, 37, 75–76
Andean people 5
Andre 105
Ant Farm and Jessie (television show) 71

anti-colonial language policies 37–38
Anzaldua, Gloria 9–10, 11
Aseya (pseudonym) 48–50
Asian people 70
Aviva (pseudonym) 27–28
Ayala, Felipe Guaman de 5

Baltazar 106
Baugh, John 40, 75–76
Bennett, William 10
Bernal, Delgado 41
Bhabha, Homi K. 11
bilingual education 3, 9–10, 13, 82
Black English 76
Black Skin White Mask (Fanon) 8
Bonaparte, Napoleon 5–6
Bourdieu, Pierre 74–75, 78
British English accents 23, 75

Cabral, Amilcar 14–15
Canagarajah, Suresh 12–13
Can the Subaltern Speak? (Spivak) 54
Cape Verde 14
Caribbean Spanish accents 31–32, 37
case studies: data analysis 25–26; participants whose first language is English 26–31; participants whose first language is Spanish 31–36; study design 24
Cervantes, Alejandro 40
Cervantes-Soon, Claudia 57
China 101, 105
Chiquita 104–105
Chwat, Sam 18
citizenship 17

Index 111

class 74–75, 77–81
Claudia (pseudonym) 35–36
Colombia 33, 45
colonial school systems 5–9
common culture 11
conscientizao (critical consciousness) 12–13
Consent Form 108–109
Creole language 1–3, 8–9, 78–81
cultural invasion 7
cultural resistance 12–15
culture 9, 11, 14–15, 58

Dafoe, Willem 18
Darder, Antonia 15
Deba 100–101
Deculturalization and the Struggle for Equality (Spring) 6
Dei, George J. Sefa 13
Dimitriadis, Greg 11

Ebonics 18, 41, 70, 76
Ecuador 32–33, 106
Egyptian accents 48–49
Elva 102
English accents 16–18, 23, 24, 27–31, 40–41, 44–45, 70, 75–76, 103
English language 3, 6, 7, 9–10, 16, 24–31
English-only movement 4, 8–11, 82
Eritrea 77, 107
Ethiopia 47, 107
Ethiopian/Eritrean accents 47, 107

Fairclough, Norman 13
Fanon, Frantz 8, 14, 54, 79
Flores, Nelson 24
Freda (pseudonym) 62–64, 104
Freire, Paulo 7, 10–11
French language 1–3, 8, 74, 78–81

Gandhi, Mohandas K. 7–8
Ghana 28
gibberish 74–75
Gilyard, Keith 30–31
Glover, Danny 18
Gross, Terry 18
Guinea Bissau 14

Haiti 1–3, 8, 76–82
Hirsch, E. D., Jr. 10, 11
How Europe Underdeveloped Africa (Rodney) 5
Huerta 103

identity 4, 11, 12, 15, 17, 23, 50, 51, 57, 60, 61, 66, 71, 81, 99
ideology 9–10, 13–14
India 27, 63–65, 100
Indian Indigenous language(s) 7

Jack (pseudonym) 28–29
Jackson, Jesse 70
Jamaica 26–27, 36, 70, 105
James 105
Jennifer 104
Jen (pseudonym) 29–31, 36, 0
Jessica 107
Joanne (pseudonym) 50
Jordanian-accented English 60–61
Josefina 102–103
Jose (pseudonym) 59–60, 61, 102
Juan (pseudonym) 31–32, 37, 107

Kamberelis, George 11
Kenya 8
Kissinger, Henry 69

Labov, William 75
language disparities 77–81
Latin American Spanish accents 33, 37
Latinx people 24, 51, 70
Leanne (pseudonym) 45–46
Linda (pseudonym) 33–35
lingua franca 6, 10
linguicism 65, 98–99
linguistic apartheid 4–8, 11
linguistic imperialism 76
Linguistic Imperialism Continued (Phillipson) 6
linguistic profiling 15, 23, 40, 75
linguoelitism 74–76, 81–82

Macedo, Donaldo 10
Malda (pseudonym) 47–48
Manoucheca 104
Manz (pseudonym) 60–61
Mari 98–100
Maria 70, 102

Mary (pseudonym) 26–27, 36, 70
McLeod, James 12
Melinda 105–106
Monica 103

Naomi (pseudonym) 59, 61, 106
narrative analysis 26
Native Americans 4–5, 70
native languages 4–5, 6–7, 10, 15, 18–19, 23, 24, 26, 37, 41, 44, 51, 70, 81–82
Negrette 101–102
Nieto, Sonia 17
Nyerere, Julius 7

Pablo (pseudonym) 32–33, 37
Pakistan 86
participants: attitude toward accent 102–103; case studies of participants whose first language is English 26–31; case studies of participants whose first language is Spanish 31–36; contradiction statements 107; experiences with accent discrimination 103–106; linguistic minorities experiencing accent discrimination 44–48, 51–52; perceptions of accent 102–103; position about accent 102–103; testimonios about immigrants facing accent discrimination 48–50
Philippines 47, 50, 85
Phillipson, Robert 6, 76
Pietschmann, Richard 5
power relations 9
Praviaj (pseudonym) 65
Puerto Rico 31, 59

Quechua 5

Return to the Source (Cabral) 14
Roberts, Julia 18

Rodney, Walter 5–6
Rosa, Johathan 24
Rossellini, Isabella 18
Rushdie, Salman 12

Santa 105
Schwarzenegger, Arnold 61–62, 69
Smith, Alison 75
South Asian English accents 28, 104
Spanish accents 9, 31–37, 102–103, 106
Spivak, Gayatri 54
Spring, Joel 6
Sri Lanka 13
standard accent hegemony 4, 14, 15–19, 24, 25, 26, 27, 32, 51, 61, 62, 76, 81
subaltern professors/students 54–60, 62–66, 82, 98–102

Tagore, Rabindranath 27
Tanzania 7
testimonios 40–41, 42, 48–51, 54, 56–66, 102–107
Thiong'o, Ngugi wa 7–8, 14
Torres, Myriam 16
"To the Margins and Back" (Torres) 16

United Kingdom (U.K.) 6, 76
United States (U.S.) 4–5, 6, 9–12, 13, 14, 16, 17–18, 24, 26–36, 37, 44–51, 70, 71–72, 75–76, 81–82, 88
Unz, Ron 10, 82

Veranda (pseudonym) 63–64
Vob (pseudonym) 44–45

Wane, Njoki Nathani 6
White females 55–56
White males 55, 56, 69–72